Quinton Coetzee

THE
BUCK THAT
BURIES
ITS POO

→

and 101 other fascinating facts
about SA's wildlife

Jonathan Ball Publishers
JOHANNESBURG • CAPE TOWN

Text © Quinton Coetzee (2023)
Illustrations © Quinton Coetzee (2023)
Cover images © Steenbuck (iStock/JohnCarnemolla), Flamingo (iStock/
BirdHunter591), Lion (iStock/GlobalP), Boomslang (iStock/FroeMic),
Chameleon (iStock/Bkamprath), Elephant (iStock/cyoginan),
Giraffe (iStock/ZZ3701), Hippo (iStock/GlobalP), Zebra (iStock/
Nataliya Rodina).
Published edition © Jonathan Ball Publishers (2023)

Published in South Africa in 2023 by
JONATHAN BALL PUBLISHERS
A division of Media24 (Pty) Ltd
PO Box 33977
Jeppestown
2043

ISBN 978-1-77619-226-7
ebook ISBN 978-1-77619-227-4

*Every effort has been made to trace the copyright holders and to obtain
their permission for the use of copyright material. The publishers apologise
for any errors or omissions and would be grateful to be notified of any
corrections that should be incorporated in future editions of this book.*

www.jonathanball.co.za
www.twitter.com/JonathanBallPub
www.facebook.com/JonathanBallPublishers

Cover by mrdesign
Design and typesetting by Melanie Kriel

Printed by **novus print**, a division of Novus Holdings
Set in Century 751 BT

Ex Africa semper aliquid novi
(Out of Africa, there is always something new)
– Pliny the Elder

For Benn and Ladoo, Clay and Keegs. May knowledge, truth and integrity be your compass – always! And to Cassie, my constant companion and 'sounding board' throughout the writing of this book.

Contents

Introduction

Southern Africa is home to an astonishing diversity of life forms, which occur in widely contrasting habitats: from dry deserts and humid forests to warm beaches and icy peaks. Without exception, every one of these animals and plants has developed an amazing strategy of adaptation to climatic conditions and habitat over time.

Since childhood I've happily nestled in the embrace of Mother Nature's wonders. I've always been entranced by the marvels and mysteries of the natural world, surrendering helplessly to their spells, which effortlessly captivated, seduced and encircled me, as a moth is drawn to light.

After completing a BSc degree in zoology and microbiology at Rhodes University, where the principles of biology were hammered into an empty head, I spent many years (surviving!) in the bush as a bushcraft instructor. I have also been a cat hunter on Marion Island, a director at the Johannesburg Zoological Gardens, a safari guide (unqualified), a professional platform speaker and a television presenter on wildlife programmes such as *Aardwolf* and *50/50*.

The hugely popular TV stint especially attuned me to the strange and unrecorded in nature (thanks to my incomparably erudite producer, Ronnie Watt). Without respite, I've been enthralled by, and indulged in, the bizarre, unlikely, remarkable or astounding biological phenomena on our planet. Every time, I was intrigued by whether these accounts were anecdotal or factual, myth or truth.

I have been driven by a search for answers. Even if you don't always find answers in nature, there's invariably a most plausible explanation. My quest has taken me to places strange and far: the unpredictably treacherous weather of the subantarctic zone, scorching deserts of the Middle East, the highest ice peaks in Russia, frozen wastelands of outer

Mongolia, shimmering plains in Africa and the sweltering jungles of the Amazon basin.

Spending time in the wild, with so many different and wonderful people, I was struck by the realisation that their interests, conversations and questions about nature were often about the same things. Whether professional naturalists or safari guides, nature-loving adults or wide-eyed children, our curiosity about the fascinating world of nature has no bounds. How often I have been asked questions like these:

- Is a zebra black with white stripes, or white with black stripes?
- Are dassies and elephants really related?
- Do frogs and toads cause warts?
- How do geckos stick to walls?
- Why do giraffes have such long necks?
- How old do baobabs grow?
- Why do flamingos stand on one leg?

And then there are the myriad of myths, legends and old wives' tales about animals that are typically seen as mysterious creatures, such as bats, snakes and owls.

I embarked on this project to answer some of these questions, and organised them into six groups – in line with the systematics of classification that have underpinned biological discovery for almost 300 years (more about that on page xii).

- **Part 1 – Mammals** makes up almost a third of the book, despite this group of organisms representing not even 0.5% of all the described species of living things on Earth. South Africa is home to around 350 mammal species, ranging from the tiny pygmy mouse to the tall giraffe, and the splendour of the Big Five in between. Our mammals are diverse, dramatic and renowned worldwide, attracting people from around the globe to see them in their spectacular natural habitats.

- In **Part 2 – Birds**, I touch on some of the extraordinary, weird and wonderful birdlife of South Africa. People have a natural affinity for birds (unlike for reptiles!), because they're delicate and harmless and often boast magnificent colours, song, intellect, powers of instant flight, and so much more. And because they've adapted to so many diverse habitats, they've developed remarkable survival strategies. Owing to their secretive (read: flighty) nature, not many people know about these behavioural traits. It's these little-known 'oddities' that I've chosen to discuss in this book in the hope that the reverence that we hold for the avian world becomes even more meaningful.

- As I explain in **Part 3 – Reptiles and Amphibians**, these animals don't hold nearly the same appeal as mammals and birds do for many people. Whereas mammals are (mostly) soft and furry, reptiles are dry and scaly, and amphibians are moist and often slimy. Indeed, the fear of reptiles (herpetophobia) is the most common animal phobia. Snakes, in particular, are feared not only because they are able to kill people but also because of the negative connotations, myths and legends attributed to them over centuries – despite the fact that the vast majority of snakes are entirely harmless to humans.

  Since this fear is based entirely on paucity of knowledge, I have approached this section with an intent not only to expose some of the little-known wonders of these animals, but also to allay some fears, bust the myths and create a better understanding of this misunderstood group.

- **Part 4** deals with a large group of invertebrate animals (meaning 'animals without a backbone') called **Arthropods**. It's estimated that these spineless animals make up around 80% of all known animal species, making them the most successful creatures on Earth. Arthropods all have a segmented body, pairs of jointed limbs and a tough outer covering made of chitin, which is shed periodically. The group spans insects, myriapods (centipedes and millipedes), arachnids (spiders and scorpions) and crustaceans (crabs, prawns and lobsters).

  Unlike most of the creatures featured in the other groups in this book, arthropods may often be encountered in our daily lives, within our homes and in our gardens. Because they don't hold much of an interest for most people (except for the prophets of Doom!), I have chosen to discuss many of the arthropods with which we're most familiar, to shed light on the little known, and once again, to assuage the misplaced fears associated with so many of these critters.

- **Part 5 – Fish** looks at the last of the animal groups in this book. Southern Africa's coastline extends over 2 850 km from the coastal borders of Namibia to Mozambique. Our oceans have an astonishing diversity of marine life, but the fish that attract the most attention in our oceans, by far, are the sharks. (Yes, sharks are fish!) People fear them universally because they are large creatures against which we have little defence in water. It is for this reason that I've chosen to discuss only sharks here, in an effort to dispel many of the terrors that surround these ill-judged yet fascinating creatures.

- **Part 6 – Plants** touches on a small section of South Africa's extensive botanical diversity. I have chosen to write mainly about trees, no doubt because of the strong allure that all things arboreal have for me. Trees have a vital role in every environment and are an essential part of our landscapes, whether in the bush or in our cities. I've realised that a landscape is only described as barren when it has no trees on it!

Trees are extraordinary for so many reasons, not the least of which is their longevity and ability to withstand untold adversity while providing refuge, shelter and food for a myriad of other life forms – including humans. Sadly, the feelings of respect and admiration we should have for these remarkable organisms are frequently absent. My hope is that this small section will encourage a greater appreciation for and awareness of trees in South Africa.

This book does not attempt to provide all the answers or give a definitive confirmation of behaviour or form in the natural world. Many answers continue to elude us, but at the very least it offers a handy guide based on my own research and that of others, and of course experience gleaned over decades living close to nature and wildlife. I've also touched on explanations towards a better understanding of the naming of our national parks, the joy of collective nouns for all creatures great and small, and provided personal insights into so many of the natural mysteries that have intrigued me and others about the stuff that's amazing, astonishing, remarkable and unexplained in South Africa's unique and varied natural splendour.

Understanding classification: The relationships between all living things

Scientists are not only keen observers but also inquisitive by nature. It's this combination of noticing how things around us look and behave and asking why it is so that forms the foundation of biologists' (admittedly limited) understanding of life on Earth.

But where do you start to make sense of it all if there are, based on scientists' current estimates, about 8.75 million different types of living things on Earth (give or take a million or two either way)? Well, you tackle it systematically (some would say it's much like eating an elephant . . .)

About 290 years ago, this is exactly what a Swedish botanist called Carl Linnaeus did – and to this day he is regarded as the father of taxonomy, the discipline of identifying and classifying living things. In 1735, Linnaeus published the first edition of his *Systema Naturae*, a volume in which he put similar organisms together into distinct groups. This thinking formed the basis of the biological classification system we still use today, in which all life on Earth is classified according to five kingdoms: the bacteria, the protists (single-celled organisms), fungi (for things like moulds and mushrooms), plants and animals.

Linnaeus realised that although a group of organisms can be described according to specific, characteristic features that are the same across all individuals in that group, they also tend to fit into a bigger group of organisms, which are similar but not exactly the same. This means that they are of a more general description than those in the specific group. And so he planted the seed for the idea that we should be able to group organisms according to different levels of specificity.

Today we have a biological classification system that consists of seven hierarchically organised levels, going from broad to specific as you move down the steps – almost like an upside-down triangle where the wide base is at the top and the narrow tip is at the bottom. The levels go like this: kingdom → phylum → class → order → family → genus → species. So, at the top end of the range we find a kingdom – a large group of organisms that all share only a few very general features. At the bottom end, we find a species – a small group of organisms that share a large number of very specific features (and are able to interbreed).

While it was great to be able to group organisms systematically, Linnaeus realised biologists (merely called naturalists in those years) needed to be able to name organisms. But there had to be a system for that, too, otherwise different people in different parts of the world speaking different languages would call the same thing by different names and no one would know what the other was talking about.

So, in 1753 he published the *Species Plantarum*, a volume on the species of plants known at the time, in which he gave each plant a two-part Latin name: the first word describing the genus and the second the species. This 'shorthand' became the gold standard and is used to this day, although the scientific community has adapted the naming convention somewhat in that the words aren't actual Latin anymore, but merely sound like Latin.

Linnaeus's system for classifying and naming organisms forms the foundation for understanding evolutionary relationships, as already used by 19th-century biologists such as Jean-Baptiste Lamarck and Charles Darwin. This developed our understanding of life on Earth even further – as you will see when you read about why giraffes have such long necks, why people say dassies are related to elephants and why hyenas are thought to be more like cats than dogs.

In this book you'll see both common names of plants and animals and their scientific names, and understanding something about how names come about in biology, you'll be able to appreciate the (sometimes heated) debates that scientists find themselves embroiled in when hashing out what the name of a newly discovered species, or the new name of a long-known one, must be, as happened to the acacia trees of Africa.

But don't get too bogged down in the technicalities of biological classification, naming conventions and evolutionary ancestry. Instead, just keep these concepts in the back of your mind as you discover the wonders of the living world around us.

Part 1

MAMMALS

AARDVARK

Is an aardvark a pig?

Aardvark is an Afrikaans word that means 'earth pig' when translated literally, but in English this animal is also called an antbear. But an aardvark is neither a pig nor a bear, and it is not an anteater either.

The aardvark looks somewhat like a chimera. It has a snout like a pig, ears like a rabbit and what looks like the tail of a kangaroo. But it's not related to any of these creatures. So where exactly does the aardvark fit among the mammals of the animal kingdom?

Scientists have thought they may be related to the South American anteaters or to pangolins or armadillos, but none of these turned out to be a good fit.

In the end, aardvarks got a special place in the taxonomic puzzle: an own order and an own genus. They're unique in this regard, as they're the sole order of mammals that has only a single living representative.

The name of their order, Tubulidentata, means 'tube-like teeth', which deserves some explanation. Aardvarks' teeth are unique in structure. Instead of the normal pulp cavity, they have a number of thin dentine tubes, each containing pulp. They have no enamel coating and so the teeth continue to regrow as they wear down.

Aardvarks (*Orycteropus afer*) occur throughout sub-Saharan Africa (hence the species name *afer*). They're solitary, nocturnal wanderers, shuffling over large distances at night, seemingly with no plan in mind, snout to the ground as they search for a meal. They eat ants and other insects, but their main diet consists of termites, which they excavate and slurp up by the tens of thousands with their long (up to 30 cm), sticky tongues.

They're well adapted for this type of diet – their tough skin protects them from insect bites and they're able to seal off their nostrils to keep out dust or crawlies. There's not much chewing of the food, though;

it's swallowed whole and ground up in the muscular lower stomach. They get most of their moisture from the insects that they eat, so they seldom drink water.

Their genus name, *Orycteropus*, means 'digging footed' and is especially apt. With their powerful limbs and feet, armed with spade-like claws, they are astonishingly efficient at digging for their food. They have four toes on each front foot and five on the back feet, and they also use their claws for defence.

A female aardvark carries her unborn offspring – only one per pregnancy – for seven months.

Aardvarks have a vital role in the ecosystem. So much so that they're considered a keystone species, which means they're crucial to the proper functioning of the ecosystem. This is linked to their digging behaviour, as the burrows they dig become home to approximately 17 mammal species and a number of reptile and bird species. These include warthog, porcupine, jackal, bats, owls, pythons, hyena and wild dogs.

Seldom, if ever, will you find an aardvark burrow that is not, or has not been, used to good effect by another creature. The veld would be all the poorer if it wasn't for the aardvark sanctuaries, dug by so few but serving so many.

ANTELOPE

What is the difference between a ram and a bull, and between a ewe and a cow?

In the smaller antelope species such as duiker or impala, the male animals are known as rams, whereas the females are called ewes. Their babies are called lambs. Larger antelope species such as kudu or eland have bulls and cows. Their youngsters are called calves.

So, where in this group of animals does the changeover from rams to bulls and ewes to cows happen?

The buck stops with nyala: males are bulls and females are ewes. All male antelopes smaller than a nyala bull are therefore called rams.

All female antelopes larger than nyala ewes are called cows.

Seeing that a nyala baby's mother is a ewe, maybe it should be called a lamb? Yet the accepted convention says it's a calf. If ever there were a non-conventional family in the animal kingdom, the nyalas are it.

Do antelope horns regrow after breaking?

Not usually. A broken horn in a young animal may show some form of regrowth, but it will usually be deformed. Horns broken off in adult animals will not regrow.

Do antelope mothers abandon their young?

This commonly held misconception probably comes from the observation that many female antelope either hide their young for a period after birth (to conceal them from predators) or, in some cases, such as with impalas, the youngsters become part of nursery herds, where the young are cared for by several adults.

As the female may be *known* to have given birth or was previously seen with an infant that is no longer 'around', it is often incorrectly assumed that the mother abandoned her young.

BABOONS

Are baboons monkeys?

Yes. They're the largest monkeys in the world.

All monkeys, including baboons, are primates. They are generally grouped into Old World monkeys (those found in Africa and Asia) and New World monkeys (those from South and Central America). Monkey species can be either from the Old World or the New World, but baboons are only from the Old World.

There are five species of baboon: chacma, olive, yellow, Guinea and hamadryas. The latter, originally found in the Horn of Africa, is the only species that has dispersed beyond Africa (into south-western Arabia).

Do the swollen red butts of female baboons make them irresistible to randy males?

A popular myth about baboons is that the bright red colour of female baboon butts and the dramatic changes in their size are part of a seductive display that male baboons find irresistible. After all, the bootylicious butt only occurs when the female is ovulating. Surely, then, it must be a sign of her sexual readiness and the fact that she is fertile?

A female baboon in estrus. The swollen, red baboon butt is an indication of her readiness to mate.

Putting two and two together, it's not unreasonable to think that the swollen, red butts are a 'come-hither' display to any available males. In fact, it's been suggested by evolutionary biologists that human males share the same attraction for the colour red, which is, supposedly, why women use red lipstick, red clothing and even red hearts to lure men.

But(t) it's a logical fallacy.

Research has shown that females with big red butts aren't mated more by the males nor that they are better mothers. Instead, studies indicate that male baboons are more interested in how long ago the female had her last baby than in how red her rump is.

Females with older babies that they are no longer nursing are, in fact, more likely to be mated. A researcher from Duke University, Courtney Fitzpatrick, wrote in an article in the journal *Animal Behaviour* in 2015 that it's almost as if the males are counting. Female baboons, just like women, are not as fertile when they're nursing infants because they don't ovulate during that time. Male baboons seem to be aware of this, and tend to choose females that have gone through more ovulation cycles since their last pregnancy before mating with them.

The red, swollen backside of a female baboon signals to a male that she is ovulating, fertile and ready to mate. For about 15 days every month, the bobo butt grows larger, ballooning to its maximum size when the female is at peak fertility in her cycle (around day 15). The swelling then shrinks again and the butt returns to its normal size. So, a big red butt is not an indication of *how* fertile a female baboon is, but rather of *when* she is most fertile.

BATS

A few myths dispelled

Steeped in myth and legend, bats have, for centuries, been associated with the underworld, the occult and spooky stuff. Just the mention of a bat, or worse still its unexpected presence at a gathering, is bound to elicit squeals of alarm and terror. On cue a brave hero will speed off in search of a tennis racket (the silver bullet!) to unceremoniously deal with the intruder.

For many people, bats are, well, just bats. They are under the impression that there's just one kind of bat, or that they're all basically the same. Nothing could be further from the truth.

There are 75 bat species in southern Africa alone, and over 1 400 in the world, including three species of vampire bat (more on this later). Bats account for approximately 20% of all mammals, more than any other mammal group except rodents. Speaking of rodents, bats are not 'flying mice', as many people mistakenly describe them. Bats are not even closely related to rodents. In fact, bats are believed to be more closely related to primates, even to humans, than they are to rodents.

Bats are the only mammals that are capable of true, winged flight. The smallest mammal on the planet is a bat from Thailand called Kitti's hog-nosed bat (or the bumblebee bat), because it's about the size of a large bumblebee and weighs only 2 g. At the other end of the scale is the giant golden-crowned flying fox from the Philippines, weighing over 1 kg and with a wingspan that can exceed 1.5 m.

Let's examine a few common myths attributed to these remarkable creatures.

- **Bats are blind.** While their eyes may be small or poorly developed and the expression goes that someone is as 'blind as a bat', these animals are, in fact, not blind. Many species of bat have excellent vision, and rely mainly on their eyesight and sense of smell to find fruit. The fact that some bats hunt by echolocation (emitting sound waves and analysing them as they bounce back from insects or other objects) perhaps supports the notion that they have no need for eyes, hence the belief that they must blind.

- **Bats get tangled in people's hair.** The reason why we know this is myth rather than fact is because bats are far too adept at flight to accidentally become tangled in someone's hair. And besides, why would they be batty enough to do so on purpose?

- **Bats bring bad luck.** Some people believe that bats are omens of bad luck. To them, a bat in the house means something dreadful is going to happen. But it's all part of bat mythology. In fact, many people consider bats to be beneficial, as they reduce the numbers of pesky insects. Some bats can eat half their body weight in insects in a single night. Nosy, superstitious neighbours you want to get rid of? Install a bat house today!

- **Bats are unimportant to the ecosystem.** Owing to a general fear and loathing of bats, their very existence on the planet is sometimes questioned. But bats have a vital role in the environment and the economy through pest control, plant pollination and seed dispersal. Bats, together with bush babies and some insects, also pollinate baobab trees. All the more reason to conserve bats and create bat-friendly environments – and encourage others to do the same.

Do bats suck the blood of humans?

Hold on to your hats: there are neither vampire bats nor vampires in South Africa. Of the 1 400 bat species in the world, only three are blood-feeding – and they're all found in Central and South America.

Nowadays, they feed mainly on domestic livestock (as opposed to on wild animals, as they did in the past before there was an abundance of livestock); it's extremely rare that they will target humans.

Vampire bats are so light and surreptitiously unobtrusive that they can land on sleeping prey without waking them up. Using their sharp teeth, they nick the skin just enough to cause blood to flow, and then lap it up with their tongues. A protein in their saliva – called draculin! – keeps the host's blood from clogging while they feed. They're so delicate and subtle when feeding that they can drink their fill for more than 30 minutes without waking up their sleeping prey.

Are bats carriers of rabies in South Africa?

The majority of human rabies cases in South Africa are associated with domestic dog bites, according to researchers from the University of Pretoria's Department of Veterinary Tropical Diseases. But, they say, there are 'rabies-like' viruses that are reported – rarely – in some species of bat and that have been associated with two fatal rabies cases in humans in South Africa. This certainly dispels the common misconception that bats are major carriers of rabies in South Africa.

I was intrigued by astonishing parallels between rabies and vampires outlined in an article in the journal *Neurology* in 1998. The article proposed that rabies and its symptoms fit hand in glove with the fearful characteristics attributed to vampires in the 1730s in medieval Europe, when people still believed implicitly in their existence. Vampires were a source of true terror in those times.

A terrible rabies epidemic occurred in Hungary in the 1720s – coincidentally at the very same time and place that the vampire legend seems to have started. Consider the following:

- **Bites:** According to vampire legend, someone will become a vampire when they are bitten by another vampire, and they will then bite others in turn. People with rabies are known to become aggressive and try to bite other people. Rabies is also most commonly spread by biting.

- **Aversions:** Legend has it that vampires can be repelled with garlic. And that they hate sunlight; in fact, it kills them. That's why they sleep in coffins during the day. Similarly, people with rabies are inclined to avoid certain stimuli, including strong odours such as garlic, and they tend to become extremely sensitive to light. When people with rabies are confronted by these stimuli, they can react in an irrational way. For example, their face can contort, their upper lip can curl back in a snarl, exposing their teeth, and they can start bleeding or frothing from the mouth while uttering strange, hoarse sounds.

- **Insomnia:** Vampires go wandering at night, apparently in search of victims. People with rabies are inclined to wander around at night, since rabies causes insomnia.

- **Becoming lustful:** Vampires are known to be amorous and lustful. In fact, rabies-infected men are prone to priapism – an erection that can last for days. Vampires are most popularly depicted as men. People with rabies are easily aroused. Statistically, seven times more men are infected by rabies than women.

- **Turning into other animals:** Vampires are said to have the ability to morph into other animals. This probably stems from the observation that the symptoms and behaviour of animals with rabies are almost the same as those of humans with rabies – they also bite, growl and snarl with frothy, bloody mouths.

- **Blood from the dead:** In light of all the anxiety around vampires at the time, it was not uncommon for bodies to be exhumed to see if they were truly dead or had turned into vampires. Exhumed bodies were often relatively well preserved, as they were sealed in coffins in the cold winter soil, but exhibited bloating owing to the decomposition of internal organs, which can force bloody fluids into the mouth. This apparently made gravediggers of the 18th century believe that the deceased had recently sucked someone's blood. Returning to reality, the blood in the body of someone who had a rabies-related death can remain liquid for some time.

It is therefore understandable that supposedly 'classic vampire behaviour' in humans may have a logical explanation. In the 15th and 16th centuries, explorers returned to Europe from South and Central America with exaggerated accounts of blood-sucking bats. But it was Bram Stoker's book *Dracula*, published in 1897, that actually cemented the association between vampires and bats.

Why do bats hang upside down?
Because if they didn't, they would have great difficulty getting airborne. Unlike birds or insects, which are capable of powered flight, most bats struggle to take off into the air from the ground. They're not well adapted for ground takeoff owing to low wing loading – meaning they have large wings but small bodies – and they also can't jump to kick-start their takeoff. Furthermore, bats don't have hollow bones like birds, lightweight bodies like insects or powerful wings – all adaptations that assist a rapid launch into the air.

Although bats are excellent fliers once airborne, it's getting into the air from the ground against gravity that's the problem. That's why they always perch on a high point from where they can simply let go for an instant, gravity-assisted drop into full flight. Problem solved! In fact, this way they can be in full flight quicker than birds, which have to work against gravity to get themselves up and away.

Tendons in bats' feet naturally pull the toes tightly around the anchor point while they're hanging upside down, enabling bats to hang about effortlessly and not fall off their perch while sleeping.

How do bats poo while hanging upside down?
Although the thought of pooing while upside down causes most humans some angst, pooing is not a big deal for bats. Their excrement is normally quite dry and resembles small, dark grains of rice that simply drop to the ground, forming dumps called guano. This means it doesn't mess all over them. Some bats can flip themselves upright for a moment to poo.

Peeing is usually done while in flight. But when peeing from a perch, some bats can arch their bodies backwards, away from a forward-directed stream, or shake vigorously (left to right) to spray the pee forward, away from the body. How's that for batshit crazy?

How do bats mate?

Mating takes place while hanging upside down, or on cave ledges or crevices. The male takes hold of the female from behind for copulation.

Mothers even give birth hanging upside down. Newborns are 'caught' with the wings and cradled against the body for suckling and protection. Some species fly with their pups attached to them. Others leave the babies at the roost during flight.

'BIG FIVE'

A marketing con?

Left to right: Elephant, lion, buffalo, rhinocerous and leopard.

The 1800s epitomised the glory days of colonial hunters in Africa. They sailed from England to Africa with fine hunting rifles and sallied forth to test their courage, daring and bravery against the 'savage creatures' that roamed the continent's plains and forests. Seeking fortune in the ivory and skin trades, their adventures and exploits were lauded back home – they were heroes of their time.

It was these first big-game hunters who determined that the most dangerous animals to hunt were elephant, buffalo, leopard, lion and rhino. Herein lies the origin of the concept of the 'Big Five'. (By the way, very few of these hunters made the distinction that we have two kinds of rhino – black and white. Should we assume they were referring to the more aggressive and temperamental black rhino?)

I find it interesting that even today, the Big Five – a hunting concept – remains the biggest marketing line in African wildlife tourism; in fact, spotting these five species is used to measure the success on a safari (a Swahili word meaning 'journey') today. I know of foreign tourists who, if they didn't manage to tick off the magic number five on their two- or three-day safari, would slink back home to Europe or the United States, blaming the lodge where they stayed, their tour operator or field guides for this 'catastrophe'. Even South Africans use this measure when they ask, 'What did you see in the Park?' and visitors boast about which of the Big Five they saw.

I find it so sad that people are disappointed when they complain that they didn't see the Big Five, and then go on to add that they spotted cheetah, wild dog, hippo, giraffe and so much more of our magnificent wildlife, perhaps even a kill – and often for the first time in their lives.

Fortunately, it does seem as if more people are becoming as enthralled and excited at the sighting of civets, serval, aardvark or aardwolf as when they encounter the Big Five. A high five to anyone who ceases to measure their safari score against the Big Five. As wonderful and iconic as they are, there's so much more to be seen and experienced in the African bush.

Have you heard of the 'Little Five'?

Clockwise from top left: Elephant shrew, red-billed buffalo weaver, rhino beetle, antlion (winged) and leopard tortoise.

In response to the hype around the Big Five and how they invariably steal the limelight, the concept of the 'Little Five' was born. It probably arose from the frustration and pressure on safari guides who become desperate to appease the primary (if not only) interest of many of their guests.

This tongue-in-cheek concept refers to smaller, lesser-known creatures who share the same environment as the Big Five and all bear a part of the name of their more famous double: elephant shrew, buffalo weaver, leopard tortoise, antlion and rhino beetle.

BUFFALO

Who are the 'dugga boys'?

No game drive during which one encounters a few lone buffalo bulls is complete without someone saying that these so-called 'dugga boys' were kicked out of the herd and now spend their time lying in mud. But I don't believe one can truthfully make this claim. Who would have kicked them out? Why would they have been kicked out? What happened at the time – was it a brutal battle or did they leave amicably by choice? I have yet to meet someone who has conclusive answers to these questions.

When it comes to spelling, I've seen 'dugga', 'dagga' or 'dagha' all being used in South Africa. Dagga is a South African term for marijuana (cannabis). In Afrikaans, the word *dagha* is an adaptation from *udaka*, used in both isiZulu and isiXhosa, to mean 'mud'. During the apartheid years, black workers who were employed to mix cement on building sites were derogatively referred to as 'dagha boys'. Buffaloes are partial to wallowing in mud or *dagha* (also see the entry on mud wallowing later). I suspect 'dugga' is simply an English transliteration of *dagha*.

Do buffalo attack their adversaries from behind?

Buffalo are included in the Big Five (see an earlier entry) because of their reputation for being belligerent, and having tremendous strength and determination. They don't hesitate to attack when threatened or wounded. Indeed, the anguished bellow of a distressed buffalo will rally the herd into a cooperative onslaught to viciously defend their distraught comrade.

It is widely chronicled that buffalo are notorious for circling back around a hunter, a position from where they revengefully 'turn the table' on their unsuspecting pursuer to stalk, gore, trample and kill him.

There may have been occasions on which a hunter was attacked from behind by his buffalo quarry. Fight or flight are the only options available to a pursued buffalo. Wounded or not, they're opponents not to be messed with. However, I doubt very much that such *encerclement* to surprise the hunter from behind is a natural or deliberate strategy.

It's more likely that the hunter had overtaken his well-hidden quarry, who might have been incapable of full flight due to its injuries. Or, in its wounded and confused state, the buffalo may have been disorientated and have inadvertently blundered in a direction that brought him up behind the hunter.

It is also said that buffalo never forget a wrong done to them. They're reputed to take brutal revenge on hunters that have wounded them, even if the incident happened years before. Presumably with a cunning ambush from behind? What goes around, comes around!

Although such calculated behaviour is not purely legend, it's also not the norm. One should also keep in mind that astute battle tactics are often attributed by survivors to ferocious adversaries, especially after life-threatening encounters.

CAMOUFLAGE CLOTHING

Can camo clothing fool animals?

The question about whether wearing camouflage clothing will make you harder to spot in the bush has raged for decades, and I suspect it's probably fuelled by the hunting industry, a sector worth billions of rands annually. It could also be because humans marvel at the fantastic examples of camouflage in the insect world, which we are often completely fooled by.

But the joke is probably on us. Camouflage clothing may be effective to humans in a military context and specifically during covert operations when we must try to conceal ourselves from the opposition in the outdoors (although I notice that for some, camouflage clothing is all the rage when going to a shopping mall).

However, the same cannot be said about making ourselves less conspicuous to animals. Even though animals do rely on their eyesight to detect potential threats, equally important – if not more so – is their acute sense of smell, movement and silhouette, all of the latter having nothing at all to do with camouflage patterns.

For some reason it's considered cool to wear camo in the bush, to blend in by looking all 'leafy', as if that is the natural way to be 'in tune' with nature. But animals do not perceive the world around them in the same way humans do. Our indigenous hunters have known this for centuries and that is why they use stealth, not camouflage, to outwit their prey. Besides, if camouflage colours and patterns according to human design really work, why don't we see any animals using this clever trick? After all, there aren't any buck with 'leafy' foliage patterns on their hides . . . Instead, they have spots, stripes or blotches on black, brown or tan hides. If anything, surely this must be the natural way?

Incidentally, I wonder if bullfighters would not be better off dressed in camo, rather than the magnificently ornate *traje de luces* (suit of lights), richly embroidered in gold, silver and shiny beads. It is said that the *muleta* that a matador so deftly manipulates to provoke the bull is red to infuriate the animal, which some say gave rise to the expression that someone 'saw red'. (I've heard people – city types – become fearful when they are wearing red clothing even in the presence of cattle, or when in a game drive vehicle and they come across buffalo.)

This is yet another myth. Bulls don't charge at the colour red, because, like all cattle, they're colour blind. In fact, the bull is irritated by and charges at the *movement* of the cloth as it's whipped around. Further evidence of this is that the bull also charges at the matador's larger cape, the *capote*, which is coloured blue or gold on one side and magenta on the other. No red there!

CARACAL

Why do these wild cats have tufts on their ears?

Nobody knows what the purpose is of their distinguishing ear tufts – or even if there is a purpose at all. But what is sure is that a caracal is not a lynx, the latter being known for their characteristic ear tufts. This common characteristic is probably the reason for the terms 'caracal' and 'lynx' often being used interchangeably. (To set the record straight: although caracals and lynx belong to the same subgroup in the family Felidae, a caracal is classified as a small wild cat, whereas a lynx is grouped with the medium-sized cats.)

There are many theories about why caracal have ear tufts, but none of them are particularly credible. For instance, it's been proposed that the tufts act as 'whiskers' at the top of the head to help the cat feel its way around in the dark, or that the tufts are flicked around to mimic insects while the animal lies in long grass, and that this, in turn, would attract birds, which the cat can prey on. Other hypotheses include that the tufts keep debris out of the ears, that they filter sound into the ears, that they are used to communicate with other caracal, or that they're an 'attractive' feature for a potential mate (think: size counts).

The truth is that nobody has a definitive answer; there may be no physiological function for the tufts at all. This is yet another example of humans' innate need to find some sort of scientific or evolutionary explanation for any and every feature exhibited by an animal.

 # DASSIES

Are the dassie and the African elephant related?

They are indeed. Dassies (Afrikaans for rock hyraxes, from the Dutch word *das*, which refers to a badger) are a thousand times smaller than elephants and resemble large rodents. Yet about 65 million years ago they shared a common ancestor, from which they've both retained a number of characteristics, such as skull structure, incisor tusks (most tusked animals have canine tusks), concealed internal testes and sweat glands on their feet.

However, dassies aren't elephants' *closest* living relatives. Instead, this title goes to dugongs and manatees – marine mammals also known as sea cows that belong to the order Sirenia – which parted evolutionary ways with Proboscidea, the order to which elephants belong, about 50 million years ago.

Incidentally, South Africa has three species of hyrax, namely the rock hyrax (*Procavia capensis*), which is the most widely distributed, and then the much less common yellow-spotted hyrax (*Heterohyrax brucei*) and the southern tree hyrax (*Dendrohyrax arboreus*).

ELEPHANT

How many species of elephant are there in the world?

Three, not only two as many people believe. Two of these species are found in Africa, namely the African savanna elephant (*Loxodonta africana*) and the African forest elephant (*Loxodonta cyclotis*). The third species is the Asian, or Indian, elephant – *Elephas maximus*. At a glance, the two African species are not all that different from each other, but how do you tell African and Asian elephants apart?

- ✓ African elephants have large ears – at least as big as the head – whereas Asian elephants' ears are much smaller.
- ✓ Asian elephants have domed heads, with an indentation running down the middle to create two distinct humps. The head of an African elephant has a single, continuous curve, without any indentation.
- ✓ African elephants have concave backs that dip down from the shoulders, whereas Asian elephants have rounded backs that arch from the shoulders.
- ✓ If you're close enough, you'll notice an African elephant has two

'fingers' at the tip of its trunk; an Asian elephant has only one.

✓ Move closer still (if you dare), and you'll see an African savanna elephant has three toenails on each back foot, as opposed to the four on each of the back feet of an Asian elephant. Interestingly, the forest elephant also has four toes on each of its back feet.

✓ The skin of an African elephant looks looser and is more wrinkly than that of its Asian counterparts.

Some people also look at the size of the elephant and whether it has tusks or not to differentiate between the two types. However, these are rather unreliable features: one, because size is linked to the age of the animal, and two, because although only male Asian elephants and generally all African elephants have tusks, it's not a given that these protruding front teeth will indeed develop in the animal.

What's the difference between African savanna and forest elephants?

While the African elephants are easy to tell apart from their Asian counterparts (see previous entry), it's a little tougher to distinguish between the two African species.

Forest elephants, which are confined to the rainforests of Central and West Africa, are smaller than their savanna cousins, which are scattered throughout sub-Saharan Africa. A forest elephant bull typically weighs in at around 2 700 kg, whereas savanna bulls weigh over 6 000 kg. The ears of a savanna elephant are shaped like the outline of Africa, compared with the rounder, more oval-shaped ears of the forest elephant, and their tusks are straighter, shorter and thinner than those of their forest-dwelling counterparts.

Their feet are also different. A forest elephant has five nails on each of their front feet and four on each back foot, but a savanna elephant has one fewer on each foot: four nails on the front feet and three at the back.

Can you tell the difference between male and female elephants by the shape of their heads?

You can indeed. The best giveaways for telling the sex of an elephant, namely mammary glands in females or male genitalia, are not always visible to an observer. So, an easy and mostly foolproof way of differentiating between the sexes is by looking at the shape of their heads.

Adult bulls' heads are broad between the eyes and tusks, and their foreheads are rounded. The heads of females are narrower and distinctly angular. Consider the shape of your hand as an example: with the palm facing down, cup your fingers slightly. The back of your hand has the shape of a bull elephant's forehead. Now straighten your fingers so that your knuckles flatten. The angular shape from the back of your hand to the tips of your fingers represents the angular forehead of a female.

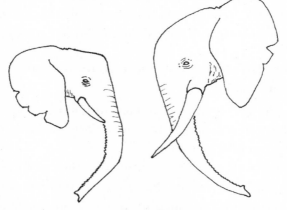

Note the angular forehead of the female cow (left)
and the rounded forehead of the male bull (right).

Are elephant bulls in musth dangerous?

Musth is a biological condition that affects only adult bulls. During this time, bulls can become 'unplayable'. (Read: more dangerous than at other times.) Their cantankerous behaviour, undue irritability, unpredictability, aggression and a fair appetite for picking a fight with other bulls (or even chasing giraffes and other animals) are because their testosterone levels rise dramatically – 60 times or more their usual levels – during musth.

A bull in musth experiences a continuous dribbling of testosterone-enriched urine, which stains the inside of the back legs. 'Elephant tears' – a thick, tar-like and protein-rich substance called temporin –

ooze from the temporal glands between the ear and the eye on either side of their foreheads. It's also often proposed that the increased size of the temporal gland causes internal pressure to be exerted on the eyes, causing intolerable pain to the animal and the consequent irrational, 'pain-maddened' behaviour. However, I'm not aware that this has been proved.

Must(h) bulls be in musth to mate?

I've often heard people say that musth is a reproductive must for elephant bulls to mate successfully, but this is not true. All bulls are capable of mating – whether in musth or not.

However, because of their high testosterone levels, musth bulls tend to be more sexually active and their aggressive state may well help them to attain a higher dominance rank than in non-musth times. Older dominant bulls within a particular area often show a high degree of fidelity, resulting in regular mating with the same cows. But younger bulls in musth stand more of a 'fighting chance' to cover cows in their range.

Musth could also be a strategy that prevents inbreeding in local populations, as musth bulls often leave their home range, wandering far and wide, to mate with cows beyond their own territory. The musth condition could therefore be a way to ensure gene transfer into other populations.

How much do elephants eat and drink?

Elephants are massive – and they need food and water intake to match. This is why they spend 75% of their time feeding, day and night.

These herbivorous giants eat about 5% of their body weight per day, with their diet including branches, fruit, bark, roots and grasses. An adult bull weighing around 6 000 kg (6 tons) would therefore consume 300 kg of plant material in a day. Food passes through an elephant's system in less than a day, resulting in over 150 kg of dung being dropped daily. This undigested material has an important ecological role: it helps with the germination of seeds that were ingested, serves as food for dung beetles and adds nutrients back into the soil, like compost.

Water intake ranges between 90 and 150 litres per day. These amounts can be drunk at once, with each trunkful of water containing up to 8 litres.

When water is scarce, elephants can go without drinking for a few days. They will travel far to find water, using their remarkable sense of smell, or dig for water underground, especially in dry riverbeds. In this way they perform another important ecological service, as the water that they uncover becomes available to other species, too.

Can elephants jump?

No, they are the only mammal that is incapable of jumping. And why would they want to jump in the first place anyway? The accomplished 'jumping-type' mammals all do so, generally, either to catch something like prey or to avoid being caught; an elephant doesn't need to do either.

Moreover, no matter how high your hopes, launching around 5 tons or more into the air and then safely landing that weight again would require a true leap of faith – it's simply not worth it.

Another bit of trivia is that when elephants walk or run, they never have all four feet off the ground at the same time (which is the definition of a jump). One foot is always safely on the ground. And, no, it's not always the same foot!

Do elephants bathe in mud to keep cool?

There is little doubt that when elephants cavort in water or mud on hot days, there will most certainly be a cooling effect at the time and shortly afterwards while the moisture evaporates off their skin. But it's unlikely to be the primary mechanism for cooling off.

Elephants are warm-blooded animals, which means their bodies maintain their core temperature regardless of ambient temperatures, with or without mud wallowing. In mammals, sweating usually allows the animal to cool off through the effects of evaporation on the skin. But elephants do not have sweat glands on their bodies to perform this function. (They do, however, have sweat glands on their feet, near their toes.)

An elephant's ears help to regulate its body temperature because of the abundant blood supply close to the surface on both sides, which I'm told can dissipate heat by constant 'flapping', working almost like a car's radiator. Apparently, elephants can pump their entire blood volume through their ears every 20 minutes at a rate of 12 litres a minute. (To retain heat on cool days, elephants perform the opposite of flapping – they hold the ears close to the body, conserving heat.)

I've been told that the dry mud traps a cool layer of air under the skin. But the opposite may also be true: the dry mud covering could serve to increase the temperature of the animal (much as we would add a layer of clothing to warm up and keep the cold out).

I've also heard that cracks in the skin help to keep elephants cool, presumably alluding to the increased surface area that the presence of deep cracks or folds in the skin provides. Again, this would only be true if the cracks harboured a ready source of an evaporative liquid, such as water or sweat.

So, whenever you see elephants cavorting in water or spraying themselves with it, they may well be enjoying temporary relief on a hot day. But the jury is still out on whether they *need* to wallow in mud for the purpose of thermoregulation. Perhaps they simply enjoy the moist, cool reprieve, just like we do in a pool on a hot day.

What are elephants afraid of?

Well, it's not mice – despite the long-standing myth that elephants are terrified of a seemingly murderous mouse in full attack mode blasting up inside their trunk to cause the havoc (I've been earnestly told!) that can lead to a horrible, lingering death. There's no truth to this. An elephant would easily s(n)ort out such a pesky mouse: think missile mouse.

However, there is a small insect that scares elephants big time: bees. Elephants react with alarm to buzzing bees and make an instant beeline in the opposite direction. Angry swarms of bees under threat release pheromones, or chemical cues, as a call-to-action for their buddies, and so the elephants know they must get away as fast as possible.

Of course, an elephant's thick hide makes it immune to bee-stings, but it's thought that they're fearful of painful stings on the soft tissue around their eyes or inside their mouths and trunks.

So evident is elephants' avoidance of bees that it is ironically being used to protect them. In rural areas throughout Africa, elephants are often shot at or killed by villagers wanting to safeguard themselves and their fields. Bees make a perfect biological weapon, which is why farmers are encouraged to string beehives onto their fences. Active hives are alternated with fake hives and strung every 20 m along a fence. The hives act as live, buzzing bells – and woe betide the elephant that rings this bell. It's a win all round: the elephants stay alive, the villagers retain their crops, the bees feed on flowers in the crop fields and the plants get pollinated.

Do elephants have a dominant side, like humans?

Turns out they do. But it's more like being left-tusked or right-tusked than humans' left- or right-handedness. Elephants tend to use one tusk more than the other, which is why one is often more worn than the other.

Contrary to common belief, elephant tusks are not canines such as those found in warthogs. Instead, they're elongated incisors in the upper jaw.

Is it true that elephants never forget?

It's probably a long shot to say that elephants *never* forget anything, but their ability to remember things for a long time appears to have a vital role among their survival strategies.

Zoologist Iain Douglas-Hamilton, world-renowned authority on African elephants and founder of Save the Elephants in Nairobi, Kenya, says that elephants are long-lived animals and that a good memory benefits them because it makes them more adaptive to environmental circumstances. For example, if elephants experience extremes of climate and they can remember where to find food throughout the year, they have a good chance of surviving.

Studies have also repeatedly shown that herds led by old matriarchs are more adept at coping with hardships than those led by younger ones. The older leaders rely on the recollections of their previous experiences, which, by virtue of their longer time in the bush, surpass the experiences of the younger matriarchs. 'Been there, done that. Follow me, let me show you how!' That's the name of their survival game.

Do elephants go to die in graveyards and do they mourn their dead?

Elephants do not go to graveyards to die, but a few things could help to explain where this misconception comes from.

For one, there have been a number of instances where people have found several elephant skeletons close together. However, a more likely explanation for this than that they go to a specific spot, or graveyard, to die, is that in lean times, starving elephants may have made it to a reserve of food or water. Those suffering from critical malnutrition likely died there.

Furthermore, old elephants with teeth so worn that they can no longer chew tough vegetation tend to frequent riverbeds or watering holes with softer water plants, and could eventually die there. Similarly, old elephants have been observed in an area containing several elephant skeletons, but these are likely random rather than planned events.

Another explanation for where the idea of elephant graveyards comes from could be that excavations in Europe have revealed clusters of skeletons of a species of elephant that has been extinct on the continent for over 30 000 years. Could it have been a mass slaughter event by ancient hunters? Or a mass die-off due to starvation? We don't know.

The legend of elephant graveyards has been around for so long that in the days of the great explorers, a few of them actually set off on expeditions to find these fabled sites. Their prize would be the great riches that awaited in the mounds of ivory just lying in the graveyard. Some even claimed to have found such graveyards. It's likely a lie.

However, elephants do appear to grieve for their dead. They have been observed covering the bodies of dead herd members with branches or sand and performing 'ritual greetings', lingering over the carcass and gently caressing it with the trunk and feet, smelling it intently. Often they even attempt to help it back up onto its feet. This behaviour may be accompanied by signs of distress.

They are also preoccupied with the bones of elephants that are long dead – smelling, touching, moving or even carrying the bones around. They certainly seem to show significantly more interest in the tusks and bones of dead elephants than the bones of other animals, even if the skeletal remains are not from members of their own herd.

Perhaps humans relate to this behaviour as we would with the loss of our own kin, and so we label it 'grieving' or 'mourning' behaviour. Are elephants showing grief in the human sense, though, or could it be, as some biologists have called it, a 'fascination with death'? Nobody knows for sure, but what is clear is that a deep sense of awareness and consciousness is at play when elephants encounter death, especially among their own kind.

 # GENETS AND CIVETS

Are they cats?

Although we often refer to these two beautiful animals as 'genet cats' and 'civet cats', they're not cats at all. Rather, they belong to the family Viverridae – mongooses. (Cats belong to the family Felidae.) Also, unlike cats, which are obligate carnivores, genets and civets are omnivores – they eat almost anything: small mammals (including bats), birds, amphibians, reptiles, insects, centipedes, scorpions, fruit, seeds and other vegetable matter.

Two species of genet occur in southern Africa: the small-spotted genet (*Genetta genetta*) and the large-spotted genet (*Genetta tigrina*). In both species, the spots run in lines down the length of the body.

Here's how to 'spot' the difference between the two:
- ✓ Look at the size of the spots, not the size of the animal. As the names suggests, larger spots belong to, well, the large-spotted genet; smaller ones are seen on the small-spotted genet.
- ✓ Large-spotted genets have light brown or tan-coloured fur, with reddish brown spots. The small-spotted genet is light grey in colour and sports black spots.
- ✓ Both species have distinct rings on their tails, but a dead giveaway

in telling which is which is the tip of the tail. If it's white, it's the small-spotted genet; if the tip is black, it's the large-spotted cousin.

Interestingly, the small-spotted genet has a wide distribution. It is found not only throughout the drier regions of Africa, but also in European regions such as Spain and southern France. It's thought that the Phoenicians or the Romans introduced genets from North Africa as pets or rat-catchers in ancient times (prior to the domestication of cats). In 2020, the first sighting of a wild genet was recorded in Switzerland!

While a genet weighs in at around 3 kg, the African civet (*Civettictis civetta*) is a much larger animal and can reach around 16 kg. It also has black spots on a predominantly grey background, but its black face mask and white neck marks instantly distinguish it from a genet. Civets are found throughout sub-Saharan Africa, except in dry regions.

Large spotted genet (left) and African civet (right).

Who would want to smell a civet's stinky butt?

The rich and famous, it turns out.

Both genets and civets have well-developed glands in the anal region that produce a strong, musky-smelling secretion used to mark territory or communicate their breeding status. Genets will often stand on their forelegs to rub scent on objects.

In the past the secretions of the musk glands of civets were harvested for use as an ingredient in perfume, and I've always been intrigued by how this anal secretion became part of classy, human perfumery . . .

In fact, Chanel No. 5, possibly the most iconic perfume of all time, apparently contained civet musk as a primary ingredient until the practice was stopped in 1998 after pressure from animal rights groups. In the early seventies, Jacques Leal, who was London chairman of Chanel at the time, was quoted in *The Provo Daily Herald* as saying that Chanel No. 5 contained the 'sweat of the whipped Abyssinian civet cat', which, from his understanding, was obtained by restraining the animal in some way and then whipping it until it gave off 'a glandular secretion'. But Chanel company itself wasn't responsible for whipping the cats, he said. 'Good heavens, no, a Frenchman wouldn't whip cats, we just buy the stuff in bottles,' he said.

Chanel No. 5 didn't contain only the anal secretions of 'whipped civet cats'. Other ingredients in its formulation included ambergris – a waxy mass from the intestines of sperm whales; musk from Tibetan deer and castoreum from Canadian beavers – a sought-after secretion from the castor sacs of beavers, which are situated very close to the anal glands. (Incidentally, castoreum was popularly used in the United States as a vanilla and raspberry flavourant in ice creams, cold drinks and alcohol!) Thankfully, synthetic versions of these compounds are used in perfumes today.

Why the hype around civet coffee?

It seems that the products of the humble civet's body functions are seen as somewhat of a status symbol by the rich and discerning of society. The focus still remains anal, but now shifts from the best perfume in the world to the so-called 'best coffee in the world'.

Civet coffee – or kopi luwak (*kopi* is Indonesian for coffee; *luwak* is the Sumatran name for the Asian palm civet) – is made from coffee beans found in the excrement of Asian palm civets, a species of civet found in China, Java, Sumatra in Indonesia and the Philippines.

This coffee craze started when coffee beans were initially harvested from the droppings of wild, free-roaming civets that raided coffee plantations in Indonesia (the Dutch first introduced coffee to Indonesia in the late 1600s). They fed on the finest, ripest coffee cherries, which tasted the best. It's said that when these 'selected' beans pass through the digestive system of the animal, they get a delicate, smooth taste and aroma because of the action of digestive enzymes that remove acidity but do not break down the material.

With increasing demand for civet coffee, the beans are no longer harvested in the wild. Instead, the civets are now kept in cages by the hundreds under intensive farming conditions, often being fed only coffee cherries for bumper coffee excreta production.

Civet coffee was first popularised in the early 1990s, when a connoisseur was so impressed with what he drank in Indonesia that he took some beans back to the United Kingdom. It didn't take long before the news spread – not least because of the unique way it's produced. It featured on *The Oprah Winfrey Show* and in the movie *The Bucket List*, where the character played by Jack Nicholson declared it to be 'the rarest beverage in the world'. Civet coffee soon became one of the most expensive coffees in the world, at one time selling for up to 100 dollars a cup!

But blind-tasting tests by coffee aficionados don't agree with the 'Best Coffee on Earth' label; it seems that the taste is not as exceptional as the hype would have us believe. 'Far from it!' say the true coffee connoisseurs.

There's great concern for the welfare of these captive, coffee-slave civets. Apart from the less than acceptable hygiene conditions under which the animals are kept, they're not properly nourished, because they're fed almost exclusively coffee cherries.

As more and more organisations lobby for civet coffee to be banned, the fad could soon be a thing of the past.

GIRAFFE

Do giraffes have horns?

Many nature lovers mistakenly believe that the projections on the head of a giraffe are horns. But they're not: they're ossicones – bony structures that are covered in fur and are attached to the skull with connective tissue (as opposed to horns, which grow out of the skull and are covered in keratin).

Giraffes are born with ossicones, but they do not pose a danger to the mother at birth since the ossicones of the baby are not yet attached to the skull – they lie flat against the head during the birthing process. Only later do these projections fuse with the skull in an upright position.

Both bulls and cows have ossicones, and you can use these features to tell the two sexes apart. Cows have thinner ossicones with a tuft of hair on top, whereas bulls have thicker, heavier ossicones without any hair at the top – similar to men going bald!

Here are a few more interesting facts about giraffes:

- There is only one species of giraffe and nine subspecies.
- They don't bend their knees while drinking; they bend their wrists.
- Okapis are giraffes' closest relatives.
- Although giraffes are generally considered 'soundless', they do have vocal cords. It's uncommon to hear them vocalising, but giraffes can snort, bellow, grunt, whistle, bleat, groan, moo and moan. At night you'll hear them humming – it's a way to communicate.
- Giraffes spend most of their lives standing up, even while giving birth. The calves fall up to 2 metres to the ground.
- Giraffes don't need much sleep to function and typically get by on fewer than two hours a day.
- Giraffes can run at up to 56 km/h over short distances.
- Like human fingerprints, each giraffe's spot pattern is unique.

Why do giraffes have such long necks?

Let's face it, the giraffe has an improbably long neck! No other mammal shares this distinctive feature. The reason for their long necks seems obvious: it allows them to browse exclusively in the top-most branches of trees – an explanation posed by renowned 19th-century biologists Jean-Baptiste Lamarck and Charles Darwin.

In his book *On the Origin of Species*, first published in 1859, Darwin further writes: 'The giraffe, by its lofty stature, much elongated neck, fore legs, head and tongue, has its whole frame beautifully adapted for browsing on the higher branches of trees. It can thus obtain food beyond the reach of the other ungulata or hoofed animals inhabiting the same country; and this must be a great advantage to it during dearths . . . So under nature with the nascent giraffe, the individuals which were the highest browsers and were able during dearths to reach even an inch or two above the others, will often have been preserved.'

But new research published in the journal *Science* in 2022 suggests that the explanation may not be as simple as that. Scientists from the Institute of Vertebrate Paleontology and Paleoanthropology of the Chinese Academy of Sciences propose that the elongated necks may be an adaptation to compete for mates, not food – the tongue-in-cheek 'necks-for-sex' hypothesis.

Their thinking goes that a long, heavily muscled neck is the basis for a formidable weapon. The flexibility and colossal torque generated by the elongated neck can be devastating when swung viciously in combat – a tactic that male giraffes have been known to use to knock out, or even kill, an opponent. The longer the neck, the more brutal the headbutt, and the greater the likelihood of winning the fight. And winning the fight elevates the social status of the victor. In this way, natural selection triumphs, with the victor passing on the best genes.

The theory is based on the discovery of a 17-million-year-old fossil of an ancient relative of modern giraffes in western China, which the researchers named *Discokeryx xiezhi*.

This prehistoric relative had a much shorter neck than modern giraffes, but a robust, disc-shaped ossicone (see previous entry) on its head. This extraordinary structure, the palaeontologists write, is an adaptation to help absorb the impact of powerful head-to-head blows during combat. Herein lies the crux of the matter . . .

Since this remarkable feature evolved way back then for the purpose of competing for mating rights or dominance (as is common in many animals today, such as the musk ox), it's not inconceivable that the inordinately long neck of modern giraffes evolved for the same reason – extreme adaptations in both ancient and modern giraffes for headbutting courtship struggles.

There's no doubt that the elongated neck of modern giraffes does allow them to feed high up in trees where others cannot, but this may not be *why* they developed long necks in the first place – it's perhaps a wonderfully fortuitous consequence of the primary demand for powerful combat.

In support of this argument are observations that modern giraffes, even in times of fierce competition for food, will not always exploit their height advantage to feed on treetops. Instead, with necks held horizontally, they'll spend almost half of their time feeding on the lower branches.

But the million-dollar question is this: if their long necks developed over time as a weapon for male combat advantage, why do the females have equally long necks? Perhaps this can be attributed to genetic correlation, meaning that genes are identically expressed in both sexes? The jury is still out.

The disproportionate length of a giraffe's neck has long been the subject of mystery and intrigue. Apart from what deductions from the fossil record and observations regarding natural selection suggest, there are also ideas that a giraffe's long neck – and the associated large surface area – could help the animal stay cool. Others propose that predators are better spotted from a lofty elevation. It's even been hypothesised that the giraffe's neck needed to extend in response to its legs growing too long so that it can continue to drink at watering holes.

Perhaps the take-home lesson here is that there isn't always an obvious evolutionary explanation for why animals look the way they do. Speculation by us non-scientific types is hugely encouraged, because it prompts questions that need investigating – being wrong is an integral part of science, after all.

But a measured approach *before* accepting simple explanations for seemingly obvious adaptations as a declaration of 'fact' is even more admirable. It's often far more productive to open the various theories for lively discussion and opinion than to declare the reason for every biological adaptation as an undisputed fact.

I suspect that the true (or most plausible) reason why animals look the way they do will continue to remain the topic of research, discussion and speculation for a long time in the nebulous world of evolutionary biology. Perhaps the 'real' reason for giraffes' long necks will never emerge.

I'm just sticking my neck out here . . .

What's up with a giraffe's long blue tongue?

No one knows for sure. Currently, the most plausible explanation is that the colouration, varying from blue to purple or almost black, is due to a high concentration of dark melanin pigments.

The tongues of most other animals are usually safely protected inside their mouths. But not so for giraffes. Their prehensile tongues are around 50 cm long and can be exposed to the sun for hours every day as they strip and pull leaves off branches into their mouths. It's thought that melanin provides a measure of protection against sunburn on the tongue while the giraffe feeds.

Their tongues also have papillae (taste buds) that are thickened and tough. This, in addition to leathery lips and an antiseptic saliva, provides protection from injury when they feed on thorny plants.

Giraffes are often seen sticking their tongues into their nostrils, and some people even claim in their ears, supposedly to 'clean' them. I've seen the 'tongue up the nostril', but I've never witnessed the 'tongue in the ear' thing.

I'm disinclined to believe that even the most prehensile tongue can rid the ear of wax. Hopefully in time we'll learn the true reasons why they probe their nostrils (and ears?) with their tongues.

HIPPO

Which mammal is responsible for the most human deaths in Africa?

Tragically, this title belongs to the hippopotamus. It's estimated that hippos are responsible for around 500 human fatalities in Africa each year (some put the figure at well over 2 000).

Conflict between hippos and humans is inevitable as both populations are concentrated around freshwater resources in rural Africa; we are cautiously and constantly aware of each another. People collecting water or washing in it and fishermen in small boats are always at risk of attack by day. By night, hippos raid riverside crops that farmers have staunchly defended. Lives are lost on both sides in this conflict.

Hippos are extremely territorial and will not hesitate to challenge an intruder in their space. In fact, hippo bulls probably rank as one of the most territorially aggressive herbivore species – yet only in water, not on land. Cows are overly protective over their young. This does not bode well when humans and hippos live side by side.

The problem is that a puny human stands little chance when confronted by the strength and aggression of the third-largest land mammal, whether in water or on land. Few humans can run faster than a hippo – they're reputed to reach speeds of over 40 km/h. Olympic athlete Usain Bolt managed to reach 44 km/h only for about 20 m of his record-breaking 100 m race.

When attacking, the hippo swings its massive head viciously at the adversary, jaws widely agape at an angle of up to 150 degrees. It's a giant battering ram charging at blistering speed with immense power. Anyone unfortunate enough to be in range of the formidable incisors and canines of up to 50 cm long will be savagely ripped apart, and is unlikely to survive the continued and determined onslaught.

Interestingly, globally elephants are said to be responsible for around 600 deaths a year – more so than hippos. But this is the figure for both African and Indian elephants. There are around 2 500 Indian elephants in captivity in that country and they account for several human fatalities every year.

Indirectly, the most human fatalities in Africa are caused by mosquitoes – and not only through malaria, as is commonly assumed. Mosquitoes also transmit other fatal potentially diseases such as dengue fever, rift valley fever, yellow fever, West Nile fever and Zika virus infections. It's estimated that these diseases account for around a million deaths in Africa each year.

Do hippos live in the ocean?

Many photos have been published of hippos cavorting on the beach or even 'surfing' in shallow waves, both on the eastern coast of southern Africa and on the shores of Gabon. This has led to the belief that hippos also live in the ocean. But this is untrue.

It's not uncommon for hippos to be found on the beach, though. No one really knows why. Some have proposed that they may have been inadvertently washed there by flood waters. However, I doubt that to be true, because hippos are masters of their watery environment. Surely they would have made their way to the shoreline of a flooded river, climbed out and waited out the storm? Besides, beach lovers don't commonly avoid beaches after floods for fear of hippos trampling sand-castles or kicking sand onto their gleaming, well-lotioned bodies . . .

Perhaps in their wanderings, especially near estuarine regions, these inland water-loving animals simply end up on a beach. When they do, they may well take a dip in the ocean, since water is their natural habitat, and also to prevent dehydration. Does it make them dippopotamuses?

Are hippos good swimmers?

A swimmer the hippo most certainly is not. In fact, they don't even float. Despite being water-based mammals, hippos don't have the normal adaptions we would expect of mammalian swimmers, such as webbed feet or a powerful, paddle-like tail. With a face that's anything but streamlined, a rotund body, stumpy legs and a short, stubby tail, a hippo is definitely not a contender for the synchronised swimming team.

So, how do they get around in water?

It's all got to do with getting their buoyancy in water just right. Hippos have extremely dense bones. The heavy bones provide just enough weight to keep their feet on the bottom. Too much bone ballast and they'll sink like a stone, expending unnecessary energy to come up again for air. Too little, and they'll always float (conceivably a great advantage if the intention is to embark on an extended river safari to the coast). The amount of air in the lungs also assists in buoyancy control.

Hippos are masters at balancing their buoyancy to remain in contact with the riverbed. This is an essential prerequisite for their aquatic lifestyle so that they can move around (since they can't swim), rest and even sleep. Hippos even sleep underwater. When they need air, an involuntary reflex kicks in, which bobs them up to the surface for a breath, and then they descend again . . . without waking up. They're able to hold their breath for about 5 minutes.

Hippos spend most of their time in the shallows, where they can walk, stand or lie on their bellies with nostrils, ears and eyes just peeking out of the water. The depth of the water determines whether they walk or do the hippo version of swimming.

In deeper water, the closest they get to 'swimming' is with a sort of underwater, slow-motion gallop using high, graceful steps. Alternatively, they forcefully leap or bounce off the bottom, propelling themselves forward – much like a Neil Armstrong-style bounce on the moon.

The point is, hippos don't swim. They can move in water only by maintaining contact with Mother Earth. This can only happen, of course, if they're denser than water, which means they must sink to 'swim'!

So, if a hippo were to jump overboard from a ship at sea, it might well be able to stay afloat for a while, but I suspect that the only place it would go is straight down to Davy Jones's Locker.

How far can hippos travel on land?

A hippo can cover up to 10 km on nightly grazing excursions. But one hippo in particular set the benchmark.

Hubert the hippo (as he was affectionately known) became famous for his travels down the eastern coastline of South Africa. In the late 1920s, he set off from his home in the St Lucia Estuary on a course due south. Over the next three years, he doggedly pressed on . . . all the way to East London, about 1 000 km away from home. Popping in at various destinations along the way – golf courses, private ponds, beaches and towns – he was wary of humans, and never had any malicious intent.

Hubert became quite the celeb, locally and internationally. When he was spotted, crowds often turned out to wish him godspeed on his pilgrimage. Everyone thought Hubert was marvellous – he'd become South Africa's national pet. So well known, respected and revered was he that the then Natal Provincial Council declared him 'Royal Game' – he was now officially protected by law from being hunted or harassed, and any contravention in this regard was a punishable offence.

Sadly, his tour came to an end in East London when a farmer shot him dead. In the national outcry that ensued, the angry masses demanded justice. The farmer received a fine of £25 for killing the most famous hippo in the world.

Only after close examination following his death was it discovered that Hubert had a closely guarded, closeted secret. Hubert was, in fact, Huberta . . .

Huberta's extensive travels had no end, even after her untimely death. From East London, she ended up in London, England, from where, unsurprisingly, she returned to South Africa stuffed. To this day, Huberta can be seen in the Amathole Museum in Qonce (previously King William's Town), thanks to the great job done by an English taxidermist with a penchant for stuffing strange animals.

Do hippos eat meat?

There is substantial evidence in the form of sightings, photo and videos of hippos capturing and killing various species of antelope, often when they are helplessly stuck in mud and unable to free themselves. These victims, clamped in vice-like jaws, are then dragged unceremoniously into the water and bitten until they die or drown.

Hippos are indeed great opportunists when it comes to sourcing meat. If they're not lucky enough to capture a meaty morsel, which is most of the time, they are known to scavenge from crocodiles, or even 'share' their kill. They've taken the kills of other predators, including wild dogs, in the water or near the water's edge. They'll have a go at eating whatever carcasses come their way – impala, zebra, kudu, wildebeest, buffalo, elephant, even the carcasses of other hippos. There's some animal cannibalism for you!

It was first thought that cases of this carnivorous behaviour were one-off oddities associated with certain individuals or perhaps a feature of a specific population. But meat eating has been observed in hippo populations across their entire range, on occasion with every individual within a pod clamouring for a slice of the pie. It's also not uncommon among individuals in zoos and other captive environments.

As meat eating in hippos is so widespread, this carnivorous behaviour is no longer considered a quirky preference that is only limited to certain bloodthirsty individuals. There's little doubt that hippos as a species will eat meat whenever presented with the opportunity to do so. Perhaps it's a throwback to their ancient pig ancestry?

Being extremely territorial and very aggressive may be an added advantage when it comes to their carnivorous tendencies.

Many herbivores, even domestic cows, are known to have a taste for meat. Duikers are another good example, because although they're herbivores, they will also eat carrion, birds, insects, lizards and small rodents. I've personally seen a common (grey) duiker with a laughing dove clamped firmly in its jaws, the wings flapping wildly on either side of the mouth. (I still wonder how that duiker actually caught that dove.)

Even though the digestive system of herbivores is adapted to eating plant material, many are perfectly capable of digesting meat. The limitation on their carnivorous preferences is that they're physically simply not equipped to be predators, as they don't have appropriate teeth, claws and so on for actively hunting and catching prey or to bite off chunks of meat.

For hippos, eating meat is a long, drawn-out, awkward affair. Carcasses are tossed, nudged, pulled, slashed, ripped, torn and mouthed as the hippo clumsily attempts to free pieces of meat. It must be a very frustrating meal.

Do hippos sweat blood?

Hippos spend their daylight hours fully or partially exposed to ultraviolet (UV) rays. This exposure is enough to vaporise any mammal unprotected by a layer of fur. Although being in water most of the day prevents overheating, it certainly does not provide much by way of skin protection from the sun's harsh energy.

Fortunately, hippos have natural 'sunscreen' on hand. This remarkable substance, which starts off colourless and turns reddish after a while, is not sweat in the true sense of the word, as it's produced by glands situated *under* the skin rather than being embedded *within* the skin (where sweat glands are normally situated). Nor is it blood. It's called (cue drum roll) . . . hipposudoric acid.

Hippo 'sweat' offers highly effective protection because it has both sun-blocking and sun-screening properties. The chemical make-up of the substance creates a physical barrier that directly blocks UV rays and absorbs them before they reach the dermal layers of the skin.

But there's more. Not only does hipposudoric acid provide two-in-one sun protection, it also contains a potent antibiotic that prevents bacterial growth.

The idea behind the use of the curious term 'blood sweat' comes from the chemical change that occurs within minutes after the initially colourless fluid has been secreted, turning it reddish and eventually brown. Its oily viscosity is just right to allow it to 'flow' over the skin and coat it in a protective layer. When it dries on the animal's skin, it hardens enough to withstand soaking for hours.

The water in which a hippo spends so much time is often a mucky, dirty affair that contains poo and a host of other undesirable impurities, including dead animals – it's anything but clean! This creates a perfect medium for the growth of disease-causing bacteria – which is why hippo 'sweat' is so important. The antiseptic effect is said to be hundreds of times more powerful than vinegar, which explains why hippo bulls with significant open wounds caused by slashing each other with their long canines seldom show signs of infection in spite of their heavily contaminated environment.

Do hippos stamp out fires?

The common myth that hippos have a predilection for stamping out campfires probably originates from real-life observations of an animal crashing into a night-time fire in a dramatic shower of embers and sparks. But has anyone ever considered that perhaps the hippo was in headlong flight, taking the nearest gap to water, and unintentionally blundered into the fire en route?

Hunters and adventurers of old would invariably set up their camps beside water, often in an open clearing. Such a clearing usually also provides easy access to and from the water for hippos on their nightly grazing excursions.

Any direct contact between hippos and fires is merely coincidental, because they're not attracted to or threatened by fires. However, being the brightest, most visible entity at night, it's also possible that a hippo could aim for a fire on its way to its safe haven in the water.

HYENA

Are hyenas hermaphrodites?

A hermaphrodite is a living being that has both male and female reproductive organs. The myth that hyenas are hermaphrodites has been around for centuries: the Romans, the Greeks, African folklore and even Ernest Hemingway have suggested that spotted hyenas can alternate their sex or are sexual deviants.

The myth probably has its origin in the observation that female spotted hyenas appear to have male genitalia and that they even get erections. However, these pseudo penises are, in fact, just enlarged clitorises (which can be up to 15 cm long). They also appear to have testicles, which are actually fused labia filled with fatty tissue. Visually, it's almost impossible to differentiate between the sexes.

Another interesting fact about female spotted hyenas is that they urinate, mate and give birth (to cubs weighing around 1.5 kg) through the clitoris – the only female mammals to do so.

Why does the female spotted hyena have these unusual body parts? Because they are 10% bigger than males, have much higher testosterone levels, and are more muscular and aggressive than males. The brutal and ruthlessly competitive nature of the hyena social order strongly favours powerful, aggressive individuals. Pregnant mothers produce high concentrations of male hormones called androgens, which they pass on to their foetuses. This not only leads to increased size and raised aggression levels, but also causes the formation of pseudo-male genitalia in the females.

Do hyenas have the strongest jaws in the world?

Although hyenas rank high up in the strong-jaw competition in Africa, they're not the chomp champs – that title belongs to the Nile crocodile.

Although I was once sagely informed that a hyena's jaws 'will effortlessly slice through a giraffe femur like a knife through butter' (which is quite a statement, especially coming from someone who's never seen it happen), science doesn't quite agree.

To determine the strength of an animal's bite, scientists use an instrument with an apt jawbreaker of a name: the gnathodynamometer ('gnath' refers to teeth, and a dynamometer is an instrument that measures power). It measures the bite force exerted when an animal closes its jaws in pounds per square inch (psi), which is equal to the weight exerted by one pound applied to an area of one square inch. Humans have a bite force of around 160 psi; hyenas close their jaws at 1 100 psi. (Interestingly, lions, which more often than not actually made the kill that hyenas scavenge off, have a bite force of 650 psi. There's a reason why the laughing hyena laughs last . . .)

Two aspects determine bite force. The strength exerted by the jaw muscles is one thing, but the combination of the strength of the jawbone, the structure, the surface area and the actual point of contact of the teeth is equally important for the delivery of a powerful, penetrating bite or to be able to crush bone or slice through meat and sinew.

Hyenas have it all. Powerful jaw muscles attached to a ridge at the top of the skull exert devastating power. The bases of the low-profile teeth are broad and squat, but the tips are pointed and sharp, a combination that allows them to get through practically any part of a carcass – bones, hooves and skin. They even eat horns and teeth! In a scavenger role, they're required to make do with the remains of what's left, the stuff that other animals couldn't eat because of its impenetrability.

At 5 000 psi, the Nile crocodile has the most powerful bite in Africa. Although a Nile crocodile can close its mouth with this incredible force, the muscles responsible for *opening* its jaws are surprisingly weak – to such an extent that they can be held shut simply by holding them tightly around the snout. That's why a wind or two of insulation tape is all that's needed to safely secure a croc's jaws during capture operations.

Here are the four most powerful jaws in southern Africa: Nile crocodile – 5 000 psi; hippo – 1 800 psi; spotted hyena – 1 100 psi; lion – 650 psi.

And although hyenas take the third spot in Africa, they only just make it onto my list of the top 10 strong jaws of the world:

1. Nile crocodile   5 000 psi
2. Great white shark   4 000 psi
3. Saltwater crocodile   3 700 psi
4. American alligator   2 125 psi
5. Hippo   1 800 psi
6. Jaguar   1 500 psi
7. Gorilla   1 300 psi
8. Polar bear   1 200 psi
9. Grizzly bear   1 160 psi
10. Spotted hyena   1 100 psi

I've found conflicting numbers when it comes to the bite forces of most of the animals listed above, especially for the Nile and saltwater crocodiles. This could be because of the size of the animals tested and then extrapolating the data for size – all things need to be equal. For example, some say that salties are capable of a more powerful bite simply because they are the bigger of the two croc species. But then, salties never evolved to clamp onto large, powerful antelope such as zebra or wildebeest, so it's not sure if the argument will hold.

Why are spotted hyena cubs born black?

No one really knows. Frankly, I never thought about this until some years ago when I spent some time watching a group of playful cubs outside their den. They were all a uniform brownish black, very different from their parent's russet colouring with distinctive black or brown spots.

Why, I wondered, do only spotted hyenas differ in colour from their parents when they're young? The other three hyaenids, namely the brown hyena, striped hyena and aardwolf, all have cubs that are almost exact miniature copies of their parents. (By the way, spotted hyena cubs are also the only carnivorous mammals born with their eyes open.)

It is often stated that the young cubs' colouring may differ from that of their parents for camouflage while they're still vulnerable. However, I would have thought the 'mottled' colouration of the adults would be *more* of a camouflage advantage than the uniform blackish colour of the cub. Secondly, the cubs begin to adopt the adult colouration at around two months of age, yet they usually leave the safety of the den only when they're about nine months old, by which time their adult colouration is complete.

It's not clear to me what advantage, if any, the spotted hyena cubs would have by being dark in colour in their first few weeks within the den, while all the other hyaenid youngsters look exactly like their parents.

This brings me to another point. So often we're determined to find a plausible reason that will credibly explain a physical feature or characteristic of an animal. While there are most certainly some adaptations that may be explained through the process of natural selection, we should be wary of thinking all characteristics of plants or animals are some sort of remarkable feature specifically and purposefully 'designed' for perfect adaptation of the plant or animal to its environment. Put differently, we should be cognisant of the human need to want an explanation for everything and our reluctance to accept that some things simply are what they are.

Are hyenas closely related to dogs?

They are not. In fact, they're more closely related to cats! Both dogs and cats form part of the order Carnivora, with dogs in the suborder Caniformia and cats in the suborder Feliformia. Hyenas are grouped among the cats. Feliformia (in other words, cat-like carnivores) are separated into different families: Felidae, such as lions, tigers and domestic cats, are true cats, whereas Hyaenidae include the four species of hyena – spotted hyena, brown hyena, aardwolf (all found in southern Africa) and the striped hyena (found in the northern regions of Africa and Asia).

You might wonder how this can be, as a hyena doesn't resemble a cat at all. It's got to do with common ancestry from a long, long time ago.

The animals of Carnivora, to which hyenas belong, appeared about 60 million years ago, and then soon split into separate lineages – the canines (dogs) and the felines (cats). Then, around 30 million years ago, the felines split into two major groups again – one line gave rise to the family of modern cats we know today, while the other line gave rise to hyenas, mongooses and viverrids (civets and genets).

Over millions of years the hyenas thrived and their evolutionary transformation was radical – today they bear little resemblance to the true cats. This is not the case for their cousins, the civets and the genets, which are still cat-like and have retained some of the feline features. That's why they're often referred to as civet and genet *cats* (also see an earlier entry).

Some people speak of hyena cubs, while others refer to the young-sters as pups. If you want to be a real clever Dick, explain to people that hyenas give birth to cubs, as one would expect from an animal that's more closely related to cats than dogs. And if you need to indelibly cement your image as a smarty pants, tell people that their name is actually spelt 'hyaena' (not 'hyena'), as per the proper scientific name *Hyaena hyaena*.

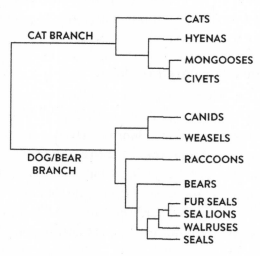

Carnivore family tree showing that hyenas fit into the cat branch and not the dog branch.

Is an aardwolf a striped hyena?

Although the aardwolf and the striped hyena resemble each other and both belong to the same family (Hyaenidae), they are not the same species.

It's sometimes assumed that the word 'aardwolf' (literally, 'earth wolf') is the Afrikaans name, while the animal is called a striped hyena in English. But this is incorrect: an aardwolf is an aardwolf, in English and in Afrikaans. (An aardwolf is also called a *maanhaarjakkals* in Afrikaans, meaning 'maned jackal'.)

Aardwolf (left) and striped hyena (right).

At a glance, it's easy to see why these two hyaenids may be confused with each other: both are striped and they have a similar body outline and ears. Yet they are very different. Here's how you'd know:

✓ You won't spot a striped hyena in southern Africa because they don't occur here; they're only found in sparse populations in the northern African regions, the Middle East and India. In contrast, the aardwolf occurs in southern, eastern and central Africa.

✓ A dead giveaway is the aardwolf's distinctive black-tipped tail, which a striped hyena doesn't have.

✓ At around 40 cm high and with a weight of about 10 kg, an aardwolf is also much smaller than a striped hyena, which is typically twice that height and can weigh more than 50 kg.

✓ An aardwolf has a more slender muzzle and face compared with the robust, broad muzzle of the striped hyena. The difference is due to their different feeding habits: aardwolf feed mainly on termites, while striped hyenas are omnivorous scavengers. Their bone-crushing teeth enable them to feed on the carcasses of medium-sized to large mammals.

Aardwolf have long been persecuted by farmers owing to the erroneous belief that they are livestock killers, especially sheep. But they don't hunt sheep because they don't eat meat. In fact, the aardwolf is said to be one of the most specialised carnivores on the planet because of its very specific diet of termites (a practice known as myrmecophagy, from the Greek *murmex*, meaning 'ants', and *phagein*, meaning 'to eat'). Using its long, sticky tongue, an aardwolf can consume up to 300 000 termites in one night.

Aardwolf also don't eat just any type of termite – they only feed on specific species found in large numbers on the ground. This is because they are not equipped with powerful claws to dig out termites or break open mounds.

 IMPALA

Do impalas stot or pronk?

Stotting and pronking refer to the same thing – a leaping action that entails jumping up and forward, legs straight and stiff, with all four feet off the ground at the same time. But stotting (aka pronking) is performed by springbuck, not impalas.

Impalas are known for their graceful leaping action, a forward-backward rocking motion in high bounces, often with their hind legs doing an exaggerated high kick into the air just as the front legs touch the ground. This kick can be so high that the animal appears to be in a head-down, vertical position, in danger of toppling over into a somersault.

With these impressive leaps, which can be more than 3 m high, an impala can travel up to 11 m through the air in one bounce – clean over tall bushes or obstacles in their way. It makes for the most beautiful bush ballet.

They perform these leaps not only forward, but also sideways, in front of or even over one another. It's thought that this is done to confuse predators, but they often seem to do it just for fun!

Do impalas delay birth till the first rains?

Impalas are synchronised breeders, which means that mating occurs at a certain time each year – usually in May over a period of about three weeks. And, as can be expected, with synchronised mating comes synchronised birthing. Since the gestation period of an impala is around six months and given that foetuses must be born at full term to avoid birth canal complications, lambs will consequently arrive over a three-week period in or around November.

I've often heard people say, 'The impalas are lambing late this year, they must be waiting for the rains.' The reasoning here is that lambs that are born in dry, unforgiving conditions will undoubtedly draw the short straw and suffer high mortalities.

While such conditions will surely have an impact on their chances of survival, the growth of a developing foetus in the womb cannot be consciously 'slowed down' by the mother. The foetus must be voided at full term to avoid birthing complications. However, the gestation period of an impala is given as between six and seven months (183–213 days), which means there's about 30 days' leeway for gestation to be completed. This suggests that late rains and little food could *slightly* delay lambing due to the mother's restricted nutrient intake, which may influence the development of the foetus. On the other hand, and by the same reasoning, optimal environmental conditions could cause lambing to occur *slightly* earlier owing to optimal foetal development – with 'slightly' implying a few days rather than weeks.

As a survival strategy, impalas are experts at concealing their lambs, even in sparse cover. So, one explanation could be that we simply don't see the first lambs that are born early in the season. Neither will we see the lambs that have been aborted or abandoned by their mothers in desperate times, because they're immediately snaffled up by predators.

The large number of lambs that we do see later in the season, *after* the rains, may simply have been conceived later in the mating period.

 # KLIPSPRINGER

What is the secret to the klipspringer's 'bouncy' hair?

Klipspringer is an Afrikaans word that literally means 'rock jumper'. Rocky outcrops, where these dainty antelope live, can experience extreme temperature variations, becoming either very hot or very cold.

The hairs that make up a klipspringer's fur are thick, coarse, springy and flattened. They're also hollow, almost resembling small quills. This makes their fur an excellent insulator (the hairs in a polar bear's fur are also hollow to maximise insulation).

It is said that the hollow fur may also have a cushioning, protective function should the animal fall in its harsh environment. It's possible, but not proven. However, there is no doubt that a concentrated mass of this springy, hollow hair does have a spongy effect – the 'bouncy' properties were particularly sought after in the past by settlers who hunted klipspringers, not only for their meat, but also for their hair, which was prized for the stuffing of riding saddles.

Why are klipspringers so agile on rocky surfaces?

Klipspringer hooves are specifically adapted to their rocky lifestyle. Their long hooves point downwards and have blunt, cylindrical tips. The small, round surfaces provide the hooves with an outstanding, rubber-like grip on rocky surfaces. It's on these hoof tips that klipspringers walk, hop and leap with remarkable agility and sure-footedness, as if 'magnetised' onto steep, smooth rocks. One could easily call them boulder ballerinas.

LION

A few tall tales about lions

Lions are historically among the most iconic of animals and have been revered worldwide since ancient times. Tales, myths and legends about lions abound. Let's look at a few that you might hear around a campfire:

🐾 **A lion's mane serves to protect the neck during fighting.**
Lions in combat viciously rake at the face and mostly attack
the opponent's flank and hips, rather than the head and neck.
Although the mane may indeed have some protective role, this is
likely to be incidental. Even though there are uncommon cases
recorded of males *without* manes and females *with* manes,
the function of a mane is most likely to communicate status,
strength and sexual fitness.

🐾 **Lions prefer to hunt under a full moon.** No, they don't. The
darker the night, the better for hunting. With their binocular
vision and an astonishing ability to assimilate even the faintest
amount of residual light, even on moonless or cloudy nights,
lions may have an advantage over prey. A full moon also provides
more light for prey to spot predators, which would make stealth
hunting trickier.

🐾 **Lions have white lines under their eyes to enhance their
night vision.** Perhaps, although it's not an indisputable fact.
By the same token, these white lines may also be a disadvantage
during the day because they might accentuate the sun's glare.

🐾 **Lions can see eight times better at night than humans
can.** I'm not convinced that anyone knows for sure what the
exact scale is. Suffice to say that a lion's nocturnal vision is
incomparably better than that of a human.

Do lions roll in animal dung, entrails or carcasses to disguise their scent?

Nobody knows for sure why they engage in this strange behaviour,
but in my opinion whiffs of excreta, intestine or rotting flesh will not
pull the wool over the eyes of unsuspecting antelope, rendering them
oblivious to the presence of a scheming predator.

A number of other theories exist as to why some animals (normally
carnivores) do this. Some put it down to simple curiosity ('Hmm,
I wonder what it's like to roll in stool?'). Others suggest that lions
do this to lay claim to a kill ('Mine, it's all mine') or that they cover
themselves in the scents to inform other members of their group

what they have found ('Hey guys, check this out, I found a clump of buffalo dump!')

I find all these 'explanations' rather flimsy. For example, as lions seldom hunt alone, surely all the lions in the pride would then have to roll in the muck to mask their *collective* scent? Imagine an unsuspecting kudu's shock at being suddenly and viciously ambushed by what it had safely concluded was a buffalo turd!

The complexity of behavioural traits in nature is vast, intriguing and often (if not mostly) not fully understood. Perhaps we should guard against assigning a simple explanation to account for inexplicable behaviour. So often, this has become the origin of myths. Besides, there's nothing uncool about saying, 'We just don't know why!'

Do lions have retractable claws?

The word 'retractable' suggests that the claws are permanently extended, and that they can be 'retracted' at will, back into the paw. This is incorrect – the opposite is true!

The claws are normally passively retracted within the paw and can be actively protracted, that is, extended, out of the paw when required. It may therefore be more correct to say that lions have *pro*tractable claws.

Do male lions always kill the cubs when taking over a pride?

While fairly few people seem concerned about details such as a lion's weight or speed, the average litter size and pride dynamics, no safari outing is complete without a discussion about the 'fact' of lion infanticide – it's 'common knowledge', after all. I suspect this half-truth is shared so readily because of its shock value. After all, humans abhor the idea of infanticide.

But infanticide is quite common among many species in the animal kingdom. It's a natural way of ensuring the survival of the fittest, providing benefits such as access to natural resources, immediate nutritional opportunities and increased reproduction prospects.

When 'new' lions encounter strange females with cubs, the cubs will often – but not always – be killed. Infanticide (the killing of young of the same species) in lions is not as commonplace as is widely believed.

There is huge selective pressure for the males to stamp their genetic mark on the pride since their tenure is only around two years, and females only give birth every two years or so. Infanticide may happen not because the cubs are considered competition, but rather to rid the female of her genetic investment in another male lion's cubs. Killing the cubs may also create conditions that enable the females to mate sooner with the new pride of males.

Besides, females that are already pregnant can mate with the new males and still give birth to young that were sired by the previous males. Or they can hide their existing cubs, mate with the new males and bring the cubs back later. Contrary to common belief, males are not able to recognise their own youngsters through smell.

Filial infanticide (when a mother kills her young) has also been observed in female lions. Lion mothers have been known to abandon handicapped or weak cubs, or a single remaining cub, presumably to increase their own lifetime reproductive success.

Are white lions albinos?

White lions are leucistic, meaning they have a recessive genetic mutation that causes the fur to be blonde to near-white, rather than the normal tawny colour.

To produce a white lion cub, both parents (even if they're tawny coloured) must be carriers of this uncommon, recessive gene. That's why white lions are so rare.

Albinism is a condition that results from a complete lack of pigmentation, characterised by pink or red eyes and noses. However, white lions may have blue or gold eyes, black on their noses, 'eyeliner' around the eyes and darker patches behind their ears

Contrary to the widely held belief that white colouration is a disadvantage to these individuals' survival because it restricts their camouflage abilities when hunting, research suggests that white lions are just as good at hunting prey as their tawny counterparts.

MATING FOR LIFE

Do some animals mate for life?

You'll often hear people saying that some animals mate for life. But in fact the animals that do so are monogamous, meaning that they have only one mate. (The word 'polygamous' means 'having more than one mate'.)

Monogamy may be a cherished value in human society, but of the approximately 5 000 mammal species worldwide, fewer than 5% form lifelong pairs. (Interestingly, beavers fall into this category.) In contrast, around 90% of bird species are monogamous.

The term 'having a mate for life' is often misconstrued in the zoological sense. It does not necessarily mean that when one of the pair dies, the remaining partner continues to live in celibate solitude for the rest of its days. The remaining partner will find a new mate . . . until death again does them part.

Several southern African mammals, including jackal and common duiker, are monogamous. So are klipspringer: they stick together until one of the pair dies. You'll seldom see the two apart – they spend most of their time within metres of each other.

MONGOOSES 🦡

Are mongooses immune to snake venom?

Yes, they are indeed. Mongooses (not mongeese!) will feed on almost anything – rodents, birds, frogs, reptiles, insects and fruits. They even break open eggs by dashing them against solid objects. They're known as non-discriminatory predators, meaning that they'll eat anything they can catch and kill. This includes snakes, as was famously portrayed by the mongoose character Rikki-tikki-tavi in *The Jungle Book* by Rudyard Kipling.

But snacking on venomous snakes isn't something that should be tackled lightly. Mongooses aren't that big – indeed, they fall perfectly into the prey size of many of the larger snakes. And venomous snakes have been known to drop an ox . . . so how do mongooses do it?

Their number one priority when attacking a snake would be to avoid being bitten in the first place. Mongooses are bright and agile, able to attack and retreat fast, and usually able to evade counter-attacks by the victim just as efficiently. But should a mongoose be unlucky enough to suffer a bite from a venomous snake, it has a remarkable chemical defence up its sleeve – a glycoprotein that binds to the protein in snake venom, rendering it ineffective. That's not to say that the mongoose might not be affected to some degree, or even die, but it is sufficient to protect it from a moderate amount of snake venom. This said, the chance of massive envenomation by the snake from a solid bite is highly unlikely.

In a nutshell, it works like this. Most snake toxins work by attaching to certain receptor molecules in the victim, ultimately causing symptoms or death. Research has shown that in mongooses, these particular receptors are shaped in such a way that it's impossible for the snake venom to bind. It's a mechanism that seems to have evolved in creatures that are frequently exposed to snake venom and need to counter its action. (By the way, the same goes for snakes – their receptors won't bind their own venom, rendering them immune.)

This finding, and experimentation with the active parts of molecular receptors from mongooses or snakes, could lead to the development of new antivenoms that may be safer than those currently in use. According to herpetologist Johan Marais, more than 40% of snakebite victims who are treated with antivenom experience an allergic reaction. Some may even go into anaphylactic shock, a life-threatening condition in which a patient's blood pressure drops suddenly and airways constrict. This is the result of a severe reaction to the horse protein used in the formulation of the antivenom.

Interestingly, other creatures, such as some monitor lizards, pigs, hedgehogs and honey badgers, also show some immunity to snake venom.

MUD WALLOWING

Why do some animals do this?

Some animals indulge in the activity of mud wallowing fairly habitually, especially elephants, warthogs and rhinos, all of which have sparse hair. Cape buffaloes, covered in coats of black fur, are also renowned wallowers.

The question is this: why would these species indulge in mud wallowing almost as a part of their lifestyle, while most others do not?

Let's unpack some ideas.

- **Is it to protect them from biting insects?** Sure, a layer of mud, fresh or dry, encapsulating your body will serve as a protective barrier from biting insects. But only for a short time, either during the actual process of wallowing or until the dry, caked mud naturally falls off or is rubbed off shortly afterwards. After all, most wallowing sessions are followed by time at a nearby rubbing post specifically for this function. Considering that the animal only spends a small proportion of its time enveloped in the mud barrier, the assumption that animals wallow in mud to protect themselves from biting insects is weak, although not strictly incorrect, in my opinion.

- **Is it to prevent sunburn?** Any animal that has evolved to survive on the plains of Africa should have developed a natural resistance to the effects of the harsh African sun on its body by now. As noted with regard to mud protecting an animal from insect bites, a mud barrier would serve only as a temporary sunblock. And besides, the elephants in northern Namibia, with very little opportunity for mud protection, seem to cope well even though they are exposed to brutal solar radiation.

- **Is it to remove parasites?** I have never seen elephants, rhinos, warthogs or buffaloes covered in parasites (although the presence of ticks, especially around the eyes and at the tail end, is commonplace).

  When I'm told that mud serves to remove parasites from an

elephant's skin, I've always wondered 'What parasites?' At up to 3.5 cm thick, the skin of an elephant is pretty impenetrable, and it would take a highly specialised parasite to get through it – unless, of course, the parasite feeds on the skin itself. Or perhaps these parasites take refuge deep inside the cracks of the skin?

However, if by 'parasites' people are referring to ticks, then I must agree that these arachnids may well become trapped within a layer of dry mud on the animal. When the mud layer is shed, the ticks will fall off with it. If this occurs at a rubbing post, well, is it necessary that the ticks be encased in mud before the rubbing process? Perhaps the ticks could be rubbed off through abrasion – without the mud?

Nevertheless, there's probably more to the story that 'animals wallow in mud to remove parasites'.

NIPPLE CLINGERS AND TAIL BITERS

How do rodent mothers protect their young?

Rodent species form an important part of the food chain. Rats and mice are preyed upon by a wide variety of predators, birds, reptiles and mammals. More often than not, their young are particularly vulnerable, especially when left unattended in a nest or burrow.

So, here's an idea: why not keep them close and take them with you wherever you go? The problem is that a rodent mom can't carry them and they won't all fit into her mouth, nor can she grab them all by the scruff of the neck. The solution? Get *them* to do the holding on.

The newborn pups of certain rodent species are completely help-less – blind, virtually hairless and immobile. But they have strong jaws. Shortly after birth, the pups latch on tightly to the nipples of their mother, not letting go of them at all – sometimes for weeks! Thus attached, the nipple clingers are not only able to suckle at will, but can also be physically dragged along under their mom wherever she may go on her feeding forays.

In our neck of the woods, shrew pups take this a step further. Besides nipple-clinging for the first few days, they also become 'caravanners'. Caravanning is when the youngsters cling onto each other's and the mother's tail! The first pup bites onto the base of its mom's tail, the second bites onto the base of the first pup's tail, and so on, forming a chain of pups trailing dutifully behind the mother. They caravan, nose-to-tail behind the mother, for up to three weeks before they're weaned.

A taxidermy specimen of a shrew caravan. Young shrew pups cling to each other nose-to-tail, forming a chain trailing behind the mother.

Nipple-clinging and caravanning are remarkable survival adaptations that not only reduce the risk of predation in undefended nests, but also increase the safety of the pups by keeping them under the close supervision of their parent.

PORCUPINE

Do Cape porcupines shoot their quills?

The myth that Cape porcupines shoot their quills probably arises from sightings of animals (such as lions, leopards or dogs) with quills firmly embedded in their bodies, especially their faces. Since it seems unlikely that any creature would willingly press its face into agonisingly sharp quills, the assumption is that the quills must have been 'fired' into the aggressor.

But this is not the case. A Cape porcupine is not capable of 'shooting' or 'firing' its quills, nor are the quills poisonous or barbed (unlike North American porcupines, which do have barbed quills).

A Cape porcupine is not all quills. The hair covering its body has been modified on different parts to perform different functions. Only the back two-thirds of the body is covered with hard quills that can be raised defensively and spread into a formidable, bristling fortress. These 'hairs-from-hell' in black and white grow to around 30 cm long.

The tail has hollow, tube-like 'quills' that are white. They're capable of producing a loud rattling sound as the tail is vibrated rapidly – used as a warning to potential aggressors.

The head and neck sport a dramatic crest of thinner spines, about 50 cm long, that can be raised into an impressive, white-tipped crest – to make the porcupine look bigger.

The rest of the body is covered with flattened, coarse, black hair. Amazingly, for a porcupine, it's all in the hair!

A cornered porcupine with quills raised and 'armed' presents its rear end to its attacker. It can run or lunge backwards or sideways towards its attacker, with the needle-sharp quill points making direct contact when they stab into skin or flesh. Once embedded, the quills are easily shed by the porcupine, leaving them lodged in the attacker (lamenting, no doubt, that it's misjudged the hair-raising encounter with such a big prick). And yes, the lost quills grow back.

It's an extremely effective defensive mechanism. Many a porcupine has jauntily shuffled away, with fewer quills in its armoury, from a pride of marauding lions, some of whom (especially younger ones) were ruefully left licking their wounds or attempting ineffectively to extricate the stout quills from their flesh.

Leopards can't resist having a go at porcupines. Occasionally they're successful, usually after painstakingly trying to flip the porcupine over to expose its unprotected belly or head. This is seldom done without any consequence to the cat – many a surly leopard has been seen trying to extract quills from its face or paws. Sometimes the hunt goes horribly wrong: leopards have died painful deaths owing to injuries inflicted by porcupines.

Porcupines give ample warning that they're not to be tangled with.

Apart from raising their quills and crest spines to make them look intimidating, they stamp their feet loudly and rattle their tails while making a loud, hissing sound and emitting low grunts and growls. Of course, it's impossible to extract a porcupine that has lodged itself in a hole or burrow with its quills facing the opening.

How do porcupines mate?

This prickly subject is a popular conversation point, but I'm not going near the hackneyed 'very carefully' or 'very seldom' answer! Some people even wonder if porcupines really do mate at all. If sarcasm were in my nature, my incredulous reply would be, 'No, they don't mate. Special, brightly coloured moths come to collect semen from the male porcupines and lovingly deposit it into the sexual organs of the females.' I'd have added, 'Occasionally, porcupines just divide into two . . . like amoebas.'

Cape porcupines are monogamous. Because of the obvious dangers that may be involved in the mating act, it's the female that presents herself to the male. She initiates the sexual activity by backing into the male with her tail, and any potentially dangerous prickles are moved out of the way. He mounts her on his back legs and, quite unremarkably, does his thing.

And it needs to be pretty unremarkable, because the monogamous porcupines indulge in sexual behaviour every day! This is necessary for the female to maintain ovarian function. But actual copulation only occurs every 30 days or so, when the female is in heat for two or three days. The rest of the time, the vaginal opening is sealed by a membrane.

In spite of her daily sexual soirees, the female usually produces only one or two youngsters (which Americans call porcupettes) in the summer months. They're born precocial, meaning they're almost self-sufficient from birth. Their eyes are open, they have teeth and their soft quills harden quickly.

Please do not be tempted to buy curios or other items made from porcupine quills. Porcupines are being killed specifically for the quill trade, and, as history has shown, any trade in animal parts is likely to end badly for the species involved.

 QUAGGA

Can we really bring the quagga back from extinction?

The last remaining quagga on this planet died on 12 August 1883 . . . in an Amsterdam zoo.

For eons before that vast herds of quagga (*Equus quagga quagga*) roamed the Karoo region and southern Free State of South Africa. Then, with the arrival of European settlers, quaggas were relentlessly hunted to the point of extinction, not only for their meat and skins, but also because they competed with domestic livestock for grazing on the already sparse grasslands. It's even been proposed that they were 'exterminated' for this reason.

The last wild quagga was shot in what is today the Free State in 1878. Only one photograph was ever taken of a live quagga, and only 23 quagga skins and mounted specimens of the extinct quagga exist today.

The word *kwagga* is still commonly used by Afrikaans-speaking folk when referring to a zebra. However, the colouration of quaggas was somewhat different from the black-and-white striped zebras that we're familiar with today. Quaggas were brown, sporting stripes only on the head, neck and front of the body. The belly and legs were white and unstriped. These characteristics suggest that quaggas were a separate species from the plains zebra (Burchell's zebra).

However, Reinhold Rau, a taxidermist at the South African Museum in Cape Town tasked with remounting the specimen of an extinct quagga foal in 1969, was not convinced. Originally from Germany, Rau was intrigued by work done in Germany to selectively breed certain cattle and horses to resemble their wild ancestors. The seed for the resurrection of quaggas was planted . . .

But the idea was shunned by scientists. Undaunted, Rau sent samples of the skin to the United States for DNA analysis. The results caused a stir: the quagga's genetic make-up was close enough to that of the plains zebra for it to be classified as a subspecies.

This was a game-changing discovery. Perhaps the genes for the brown colour and unique striped patterns of the quagga were not buried with its extinction, but continue to live on within the genes of the plains zebra? By unlocking these genes though selective breeding of plains zebras, Rau and his ever-growing band of supporters believed that they could bring the quagga back to life.

It seemed like pure science fiction. So much so that American author and filmmaker Michael Crichton picked up on the concept of the quagga's resurrection in his *Jurassic Park* and *The Lost World* novels to justify his theory that dinosaurs could be recreated through cloning.

The Quagga Project kicked off in the 1980s, the plan being to recreate quaggas through selective breeding of modern plains zebras. A few years later, the admirable dream of an ambitious team of scientists and enthusiastic supporters was well underway on land outside Cape Town. It started off with a handful of plains zebras that had been carefully selected because of their brownish colouration and reduced striping. The goal was that each new generation of selectively bred foals would more closely resemble the colouration of extinct quaggas – stripe by (lack of) stripe! After more than three decades, the results are striking, and the animal sure looks more quagga-like than zebra-like.

Rau quaggas on a plain in the Western Cape.

But are they quaggas or simply plains zebras that are quagga look-alikes?

Critics and naysayers are sceptical and they argue that the Quagga Project will never be able to produce a real quagga, insisting that the genetics cannot ever be exactly the same. What about ecological adaptations or behavioural peculiarities that may have been unique to the original quagga so long ago? 'A quagga cannot be defined by its colouration alone!' they cry.

But proponents of the project fully accept the controversial criticism with the approach 'Is the devil in the detail really what it's all about?' Isn't it better, they reason, to do something than to do nothing at all, in an attempt to rectify the irreversible slaughter of a species 150 years ago? Wouldn't it be fabulous to witness herds of quaggas within a reserve, once again roaming the plains as they used to even if they're not genetically identical to quaggas?

This controversy is why the quagga stock are today called Rau quaggas (in honour of Reinhold Rau, who died in 2006). Hopefully this name distinction will partially appease the detractors and purists.

By the way (and I'm not suggesting a direct comparison here), I couldn't help thinking about the many wild game species nowadays that are being bred selectively as colour variants for the hunting industry in South Africa – black springbuck, black impala and golden wildebeest, to name a few. Critics call them 'unnatural freaks'.

The Quagga Project is not the same in my opinion. How can anyone not commend those committed to furthering our understanding and knowledge of genetics, the relationships between extinct and extant species, and the possible avoidance of the threat of extinction in time to come?

RATS

Are there giant rats in South Africa?

Yes, African giant rats have attracted attention of late owing to their ability to sniff out landmines and diseases such as tuberculosis.

They're also called southern giant pouched rats. This name conjures up a few misleading assumptions. Firstly, that they occur in the south of South Africa. Instead, they actually occur only in the north of the country, but it's the southern part of their range, which extends northwards into sub-Saharan Africa.

Secondly, they're not gigantic, like one would expect from a horror movie. They measure around 75 cm from the nose to the tip of the tail, of which the tail makes up over half. They weigh in at over a kilogram.

Thirdly, there's the pouch. We're inclined to associate pouches with marsupials, such as kangaroos, which have a handy pocket to carry around their babies after a premature birth. There are no marsupials in Africa. The pouch in this animal's name refers to cheek pouches, used to carry food or anything else of value – think of it as a backpack in their mouth. Hamsters also do this.

Because they're nocturnal and live in densely vegetated areas, they're seldom seen. But this does not prevent them from being hunted as a prized delicacy throughout their range. (Yum, giant poached rat for dinner tonight!)

Despite their big size and, well, being rats, they're endearing creatures that are easily tamed. On the African continent they are commonly kept as pets and in the past, they were a popular import in the pet trade in the United States and United Kingdom.

They became celebs in Africa when they were first trained to sniff out landmines. Because they're affable, intelligent creatures with an extraordinary sense of smell, they're without equal in their ability to perform this task. Being lightweights, they don't activate the explosives as they scurry about, feverishly sniffing for traces of explosive agents. They're much faster and more efficient at finding explosives than humans are, with no risk to human life. They can reliably sweep an area the size of a tennis court in just 20 minutes, marking the presence of an explosive by scratching the soil above it for the bomb squads geared to remove the mines.

The same job could take a human minehunter up to four days using a metal detector. The trick, it seems, is that rats don't get sidetracked by false alarms in the form of bits of buried scrap metal . . . only explosives get their undivided attention.

Giant rats have been responsible for the successful clearing of thousands of potentially lethal landmines and other unexploded items in Angola, Mozambique, Tanzania and Cambodia. They have also been trained to sniff out tuberculosis infections in humans far quicker than can be achieved in laboratory tests.

RHINO

Do rhinos stamp out fires?

This is another myth often recounted around campfires. Perhaps it originated in Malaysia, home of the legendary Badak api, or fire rhino. Badak api, it is said, took it upon itself to stamp out any fires that were lit in the forest. In modern times the myth has been further popularised in the *The Simpsons*, the cult television programme that ran for 31 years. Interestingly, *The Simpsons'* author claims (rather unwisely) that the series 'helped create a generation of wise guys . . .'

Then in the 1980s, South African filmmaker Jamie Uys came along with the movie *The Gods must be Crazy*, which included a scene with a rhino stomping out a campfire. This movie was released in 45 countries and became an instant hit, breaking box-office records in Australia, Europe and South America. It was the highest-grossing movie in Japan in 1982 and the highest-grossing non-American produced movie in the United States in 1984. Little wonder it became a well-known 'fact' that rhinos 'stomp out fires'.

I've even heard of a tourist who refused to join his friends huddled around the campfire, placing his chair some distance away instead, in case a fire-fighting rhino arrived to quell the blaze. Good thinking, Bond! But of course, it never happened.

Does dehorning help to save rhinos from poachers?

Dehorning on its own is not sufficient – it must be done in conjunction with other intensive antipoaching measures.

Dehorning is not only a costly operation with regard to labour, veterinary input and air and ground support, but also a tricky business –

cutting too close to the skull can lead to infection and even the animal's death. The horn never stops growing. Once cut, the stump immediately starts to regrow, at a rate of around 12 cm per year. Owing to the promise of high returns from rhino horn, even the partial stumps of previously dehorned rhinos are not ignored by poachers. This means the horn regrowth needs to be trimmed regularly in order to prevent the rhino from being targeted.

But it seems that even dehorned rhinos have been shot dead. This senseless slaughter may seem like a pointless exercise to you and me, but from the poacher's perspective, there may be a sound – albeit alarming – reason.

Rhino poaching is a dangerous occupation. Poachers are constantly up against trained, well-organised antipoaching forces specifically mobilised to hunt them down using hi-tech equipment and aircraft. They face extreme risks. In fact, poachers caught in the act put their lives on the line to the extent that gun battles have accounted for deaths on both sides.

In general, poachers therefore favour a stealthy 'quick-strike' strategy. However, the poacher could discover that the rhino that they had been tracking for some time and at huge risk has been dehorned – a massive blow to the objectives of the poacher, for a potentially lethal risk was taken, which now will have little or no return. And that's why, I'm told, poachers will shoot a dehorned rhino – to ensure that that particular 'no-worth' animal can never be tracked again. This is obviously a calculated move, as the sound of the shot may, in itself, reveal their presence.

Dehorning should therefore be seen not only as a measure to protect the life of a rhino but even more so as a way to rid the environment of horn material, making it more difficult to find rhino horn in the wild by reducing the amounts 'on the hoof', and therefore lessening the trade. But then, some ask whether this will not simply increase the price of rhino horn, making it even *more* sought after for illegal trade.

For now, dehorning is a desperate, interim measure to buy time for these majestic creatures that are persecuted so relentlessly and brutally for financial gain, until the long-standing dilemma on how to stop the demand for rhino horn can be solved.

There have been concerns about the dehorning of rhino having negative effects on their social behaviour, their ability to protect themselves or their young, and foraging. This does not seem to be the case, although more research needs to be done in this regard.

Is rhino horn an aphrodisiac?

Rhino horn is made up of keratin, the same protein that our hair and nails are made of. There's no evidence whatsoever that it contains any aphrodisiac properties. I understand that rhino horn can play a part in sexual gratification, but this would require the horn to be strapped on.

Furthermore, the well-accepted notion that it is sought after as an aphrodisiac is also not quite true. The indiscriminate slaying of rhinos for use in the East as a natural Viagra is by no means the primary driver for the rhino horn trade.

According to TRAFFIC, a conservation organisation focused on recording wildlife trade, consumer demand for rhino horn comes almost exclusively from Asian markets, mostly China and Vietnam. A 2018 article in the journal *Tropical Conservation Science* notes that the horn is coveted mainly for two reasons: for use in traditional medicines and for its high financial value among some wealthy Asians. It's used as a status symbol to portray success and extreme wealth or to give as an extravagant gift in the form of carvings or jewellery. It can even be powdered and stored in an elaborate ampoule.

The generalised perception that it's used by 'the Chinese' (as a population!) lacks perspective. Seeing that rhino horn is more valuable than diamonds, gold or cocaine, it's affordable only to the 'millionaire market' in Asia, knocking the general population completely out of the financial equation. Only the very rich are able to boast about drinking potions mixed with rhino horn to cure hangovers. One would think that the calibre and 'worldliness' attributed to individuals or businessmen who have attained a disproportionate share of wealth would mean that they would know better or be educated enough to afford medically proven alternatives to cure their ailments, whatever they might be. Still, within this group there is a minority who believe in the traditional 'magic' attributed to rhino horn to treat aches and pains, including cancer, gout, rheumatism and high blood pressure. It is even used by some to purge bad spirits.

Rhino horn is also in high demand in Yemen. It's coveted as the handles for the Jambiya daggers traditionally worn by Yemeni men. In this society, antique daggers with rhino-horn handles can sell for up to a million US dollars.

 # SHREWS

Are elephant shrews related to elephants?

Oddly, they are distantly related to elephants, but they are not shrews. (And by the way, shrews are not rodents – they're related to moles and hedgehogs. Hedgehogs are not related to porcupines, though. Taxonomy is a little messy, I know . . .)

Elephant shrews (also called sengis – from a monetary unit in the Democratic Republic of the Congo) derive their name from looking like shrews and their long, supple noses resembling tiny elephant trunks. But their snouts are nothing like elephant trunks – they're far less flexible and cannot be used to pick anything up.

Elephant shrew ancestry has long been a mystery: these animals have legs like an antelope, long and spindly relative to their body size; they have a trunk like an elephant; a long tongue like an anteater; teeth like a herbivore and a tail like a mouse. But recent evidence suggests that they are descended from an ancient group of African mammals whose relatives include elephants, hyrax, sea cows and aardvark.

They're extremely territorial and will not hesitate to challenge any trespasser. Intruders are immediately and viciously repelled with much kicking, snapping and squealing in a flurried blur of entangled opponents. Presumably the loser retreats with his nose out of joint.

Unlike other small mammals, they feed during the day, eating invertebrates that live in leaf litter, such as ants, termites, spiders and beetles. They're monogamous and can produce two or three precocial pups around four times a year.

SKUNKS

Do skunks occur in southern Africa?

No, true skunks are found only in the Americas. But in southern Africa we do have something that looks (and smells) very similar, and it's often incorrectly called the African skunk.

In South African literature, it's also referred to as the striped polecat or zorilla. The name 'zorilla' comes from the word *zorro*, meaning 'fox' in Spanish, which makes it, to my mind, inappropriate. I'm therefore inclined to favour the term 'striped polecat'. And in case you thought that the word 'pole' refers to the polar regions and is therefore equally inappropriate, it's not: it actually derives from the old French word *poule*, meaning 'chicken' – the chicken-eating cat. Maybe just as inappropriate?

Striped polecats are omnivorous and are found throughout southern Africa, especially in the drier regions. They are feisty little creatures that will, without hesitation, adopt an impressive defence display by turning broadside to the threat with body hair and tail fully erect. This is often accompanied by the ejection of a foul-smelling liquid from their anal glands – even lions are known to have retreated in disgust!

Sadly, these endearing little warriors are often found killed on the roads, most likely because they bravely direct their threat display at oncoming vehicles, rather than beating a retreat.

STEENBOK

Do steenbok bury their poo?

Yes! And not only do they bury their poo, but the females also eat the poo and drink the urine of their babies.

Steenbok have special toilet areas (latrines) within their territories. Urination and defecation are always linked. The animal scrapes an area with its front feet and urinates on the patch. It then deposits its dung on top of the urine and scrapes again with its front feet to place a layer of sand on the excrement. They are the only bovid known to do this. (Bovids are ruminant animals with cloven hooves; antelope, sheep, goats, cattle, buffalo and bison are bovids.)

Some people suggest that steenbok bury their dung to conceal their scent from predators. But I disagree. After all, steenbok are highly territorial, readily marking their territories with urine, dung and various glandular secretions. They've even been known to use roads and telephone lines as territorial boundaries.

If anything, the 'burying' of their excrement could perhaps help to preserve or retain territorial odours for a longer period, as the odour-releasing dung or urine may not dry out as rapidly when buried.

But there's more. Steenbok lambs are born after a gestation period of about seven months. They're immediately and carefully hidden in the undergrowth for the next three to four months. The mother visits the baby only briefly in the mornings and evenings to groom and feed it. During these contacts, she will eat the faeces and drink the urine of the infant, possibly in an effort to reduce odours at the hiding place that may attract predators.

These tiny antelope average around 12 kg in weight and are abundant throughout southern Africa. Only the males have horns. The name could be derived from the Afrikaans word *steen*, meaning 'brick or rock' – a reference to the brownish-red colour of the animal. The underparts are white.

Another fascinating fact about steenbok is that, unlike other antelopes, which need to drink water every day, they seldom do. In fact, because of the high moisture content of their diet, steenbok can live independently of free water.

 # VERVET MONKEYS

Why do these monkeys have blue nuts?

Nobody knows for sure, but the 'blue balls' are not because they're not getting lucky.

Many primate species exhibit bright patches of skin colour. Often this is due to hormonal shifts. That's why a female baboon has a red booty (see page 6).

But not so in male vervets. The blue scrotum (more turquoise, actually) is an illusion, a trick of the light, because there's no blue pigment in the skin at all. The blue that we see is caused by the Tyndall effect – the scattering of light by particles in its path.

In a nutshell, the skin of the scrotum consists of collagen fibres that are arranged in an exceptionally ordered manner. In fact, this particular arrangement of collagen fibres results in only the blue wavelengths of the spectrum of visible light being reflected, while all the other colours of light striking that area (such as red or green) are absorbed. The result is that only the blue light makes it to our eyes, and that's why the monkey's nuts look blue to us. So perfect is this collagen layout that if the distance between or the size of the fibres were to vary just a fraction of a millimetre, a different colour would be reflected.

What is the reason for this phenomenon? In vervets, it's thought that females may be more attracted to a fine set of blue-hued family jewels . . . the bigger and bluer, the better! It is possibly a natural selection advantage that signals health, strength and status.

WARTHOG

Why do warthogs have warts?

They're actually not warts at all! In humans, warts are raised bumps on our skin that are caused by a strain of the human papillomavirus. But other than a warthog's 'warts' being raised bumps on the skin, there's little similarity.

A warthog's warts are tough, protective outgrowths that are made up of bone and cartilage. It is interesting to me that most people have never realised that male warthogs have more warts than female warthogs. Males (boars) have four warts – two large ones below the eyes and two smaller ones above the mouth. Females (sows) only have two smaller warts below their eyes. (Counting the warts is a good way of identifying the sex of a warthog: boars have four, sows have two.)

Their function is certainly not an attempt at winning a beauty pageant, so why have them then?

Fighting! The warts offer protection to the males when they're jousting with each other for mating rights during mating season. Male warthogs fight with their heads pressed together hard, at the same time each delivering vicious blows and swipes at the opponent's head from any angle. Their bottom tusks are razor sharp, capable of inflicting serious wounds. Predators know this all too well – there are even reports of warthogs that have disembowelled their attacker.

The power and brutality exhibited by two male warthogs in combat is a most frightening spectacle. Going in warts an' all, ruthlessly hacking and head-slashing each other, one would expect the merciless brawl to end in a profuse spilling of blood, guts and gore. But amazingly, this seldom happens. More often than not, when the dust settles, they part ways. Incredibly, with barely a scratch. It seems that the warts may indeed shield their heads from injury.

Since females don't generally engage in fighting, there's no need for additional protection. And that is, no doubt, why they have fewer warts.

What is unique about the desert warthog?

Unbeknown to many, there are actually two species of warthog in Africa – the common warthog (*Phacochoerus africanus*), which has four subspecies, and the desert warthog (*Phacochoerus aethiopicus*). The desert warthog has two subspecies, one of which went extinct in the 1870s. (It was known as the Cape warthog [*Phacochoerus aethiopicus aethiopicus*] and occurred here in South Africa and possibly also in Namibia.)

Common warthogs are widespread in sub-Saharan Africa, while desert warthogs are confined to the Horn of Africa. The warthog is one of Africa's least-known large mammals.

There are a number of features by which you can distinguish a desert warthog from its common cousin in the field, but I'm particularly taken by the desert warthog's ear tips, which are always bent backwards, and the peculiar hook-shaped warts on their faces.

Desert warthog. Note the hook-shaped warts and back-swept ears.

Do warthogs really scream when charging an electric fence?

Even though they have unfortunately been labelled one of the ugliest animals in their kingdom, warthogs are much-loved creatures. Kids love Pumbaa, the warthog character that was immortalised in the animated movie *The Lion King*. Warthogs even bring a smile to the faces of adults when they're spotted in the bush. Their comical retreats, with tail held stiff and aloft like an aerial, never fail to elicit a giggle or two. Lions, leopards and other large predators love them too, but for a different reason . . .

When I'm in the bush with a group of people and we encounter warthogs, I'm often regaled with the story of a screaming warthog by a member of our party. My good friend Duncan Macgregor, an outdoors-man with whom I've spent many happy hours fishing on the sea and on game drives in the bush, really loves to tell this tale. The story is supposed to convey something about warthogs' feisty nature, because they're renowned for their insurmountable grit and pig-headed deter-mination, especially the resolute willpower they muster to get through any barrier fence – going either under it or directly through it.

Duncan's story is of a gutsy warthog that had had a previous alter-cation with an electric fence, and describes how he takes on another. Not an animal to give up or to be repelled by a challenging obstacle, the warthog supposedly takes its time to carefully size up the offending fence from a distance. Then, mustering every iota of its strength, it launches itself into a formidable, blazing charge directly at the fence, intending to smash through it using brute strength.

Fully aware of the electric shock it's about to endure, the warthog, with eyes tightly closed in a terrified yet determined grimace, lets out an almighty scream in anguished anticipation of what's to come. Then, in a cloud of dust, twanging wires, rattling fence posts and an earth-shattering howl, it explodes through the fence. On the other side, it's 'aerial up' before it jauntily trots away, as if nothing had happened.

Is this a true tale? It's always someone else who told the story. But nobody seems to know with certainty of anyone who has reliably actu-ally seen (or rather, heard) a warthog scream as it charges an electric fence.

It doesn't matter, really, because I don't even consider this engaging tale in the 'myth' category. It's simply fun – a lovely story that tells of the doggedness of one of our most endearing animals. Everyone relates to the hollering charge and the anticipation of the dreaded shock – it's guaranteed to raise a laugh and engender a greater love for the bush and its inhabitants.

On a more serious note: South Africa is revered for the diversity of wildlife that is so abundant in the country's national parks, reserves and private game farms. In fact, there are more animals under conser-vation management in private hands than in all our national parks. To keep wildlife safely in and undesirable threats, such as poachers, dogs and so on out, thousands of kilometres of electric fences have been erected across the country.

Sadly, this fencing is responsible for much distress and many unintended fatalities among non-target animals, notably tortoises and pangolins. More often than not, an electrified tripwire strung at a height of 15 cm above the ground is the culprit. The unkind jolt it delivers shocks most intruders into beating a hasty retreat. However, it's not in the nature of all animals to respond in this way.

Upon innocently barging into the tripwire, the initial shock a tortoise receives causes it to withdraw instantly into its shell. Immobile now but still touching the wire, the pulsing shocks continue, on and on and on, relentlessly, until the tortoise eventually dies of heart failure.

The same thing happens with pangolins. The initial shock causes them to roll into a protective ball, sometimes wrapping around and encircling the tripwire. Continually defending against the repeated shocks, the pangolin remains defensively coiled up in contact with the wire until it dies. According to the conservation organisation Pangolin. Africa, studies show that as many as 1 000 pangolins are killed in this way every year, making fence electrocutions the greatest threat to pangolins in southern Africa, even more so than poaching.

Leguaans (monitor lizards) and snakes, including pythons and mambas, have been found shocked to death, their jaws still locked firmly onto the tripwire as they attempted to bite back in defence. In his Master's study in 2008, Andrew Beck from the University of the Witwatersrand (Wits) estimated that 21 000 reptiles were killed annually in this way. Who knows how many thousands of kilometres of additional potentially lethal electric fences have been erected since then, vastly increasing the number of deaths of non-target species annually?

Some say the threat posed to these species is more devastating than veld fires and poaching, and that this 'conservation' practice has the potential to wipe out entire populations. It's not unlikely that within smaller fenced areas, most individual animals will at some stage come into contact with the fence.

Thankfully, there is some awareness in the electric fencing trade about this issue. I was encouraged when I raised this matter with my friend Neil Maclaughlin, who is probably the biggest and most experienced fencing contractor on the continent. He is also a nature lover and conservationist, and is therefore acutely aware of the dangers of electric fencing on non-target species. Working hand in hand with reptile, pangolin and other conservation groups, Neil has redesigned and adopted non-lethal fencing measures to allay the devastating effect of electric fences. 'I haven't lost a tortoise in years,' Neil told me.

 # WATERBUCK

Does the stench of waterbuck repel predators?

It's a commonly held belief that the musky 'stink' of waterbuck renders their meat unpalatable to predators and humans. I've heard people say that not even lions or crocodiles will eat waterbuck. I also know of hunters who swear blind that the flesh of this animal is inedible.

This is a myth. In fact, waterbuck are a favoured prey of lions. They're also happily eaten by crocodiles, spotted hyenas, wild dogs, leopards and cheetahs. And then there's the human hunting fraternity (including poachers) that specifically target waterbuck for their meat. The 'trick', they say, is to prevent the skin from coming into contact with the meat while the animal is being skinned. Simple as that.

The natural function of this musky exudate is still not fully understood. Some say it waterproofs the coats of these water-loving animals, while others suggest that the odour repels biting flies. In my opinion, the musky smell is not that unpleasant, but has sweetish, earthy undertones.

Waterbuck don't live *in* water, but are always near it.

WEASELS

Do they occur in South Africa?

Yes. African weasels are the second-smallest carnivores on the continent, the smallest being dwarf mongooses. African weasels are only about 30 cm long and weigh around 300 g. They're striking little animals with contrasting black-and-white stripes running down their long, slender bodies. The head and tail are white on top. They occur in the southern and eastern parts of South Africa, and feed mostly on small rodents. Like genets and civets, they are capable of ejecting a foul-smelling fluid used as a defence mechanism from their anal glands.

African weasels are very rarely encountered because of low population densities due to factors like habitat loss and traditional medicine uses. Their numbers are believed to be declining.

But what African weasels lack in size and number, they make up for in other ways . . . they copulate for 60 to 80 minutes at a time – one of the longest copulation periods among the African mammals. When it comes to size versus effort, this firm and hard-earned distinction deserves a standing ovation!

WILD DOGS

Do wild dogs communicate by sneezing?

Indeed. A pack of African wild dogs is led by an alpha male and female, who do most of the breeding (occasionally, the beta female may have a litter of pups). Already, this sounds very much like a despotic, authoritative arrangement within the pack – a case of 'Toe the line, or else!' However, research on wild dogs in Botswana shows that the assumed rule may not be as autocratic as it sounds – the decision to go on a hunt (or not) is made by individuals casting their vote . . . by sneezing.

Before the pack embarks on a hunt, they perform an animated ritual called a 'social rally'. It's initiated by a single dog and transforms the pack into a highly energised flurry of wagging tails, touching heads, nuzzling, and animated dashes and sprints. The rally ends either with the dogs setting off excitedly on a hunt or the frenzy evaporates and the dogs go for a nap . . .

How was the final outcome decided? The pack members seem to use sneezes to show their acceptance for the proposal by another dog to go hunting. The greater the number of sneezes, the greater the chances that the pack will set off on a hunt, with the frequency of sneezes peaking just before the dogs set off. It's as if a vote has been cast, and the result has been accepted by the pack.

The researchers noticed not only that the likelihood of a hunt increased with increased sneezing, but also that the higher an individual's rank in the pack, the more their sneeze counted. When the top dogs initiated the rally, only three sneezes were required to get the hunt going. If lower-ranking members kicked off the proposal, it took ten sneezes to initiate the hunt.

To hunt or not to hunt – it's much ado about achoo!

Are wild dogs endurance hunters that rely on teamwork for success?

Popular literature and wildlife documentaries portray African wild dogs as the ultimate pack hunters. They're famous for their teamwork and for using the renowned 'relay' strategy – when rested or fitter dogs take over the chase from their tired team members in the front. This tactic is applied relentlessly by the pack, together with remarkable endurance and stamina as they wear down their prey, which is incapable of matching the persistent pursuit. It's said that in this way, the dogs can keep up the blistering pace for kilometres, while the fleeing target cannot. Their teamwork and endurance have contributed to their reputation for being much more successful hunters than lions or leopards.

But is this really so? Researchers from the Royal Veterinary College observing a particular pack of wild dogs in Botswana suggest otherwise. They fitted the dogs with collars so that their acceleration, speed and individual positions could be monitored on a hunt, especially when they moved out of sight.

The findings debunked almost everything previously believed about wild dogs' hunting strategy. There was no evidence of any teamwork or coordination during the hunt, chases were over short rather than long distances and their killing success rate was only around 16%.

In fact, the research suggests that the hunts were everything but organised. Data from over 1 000 chases showed that although most of the dogs ran in the same direction on a chase, they did not exhibit strategic manoeuvres to block or flank prey. Even when the entire pack rallied for a hunt, not all the dogs ran together or at the same time – they ended up scattered in different locations afterwards, signalling that they weren't targeting the same prey.

This is very different from the 'tactically brilliant' endurance hunting strategies so often attributed to wild dogs. But it does not suggest that they are inefficient hunters. In fact, their hunting style is extremely efficient. The research showed that because wild dogs are so opportunistic and almost always willing to have a go at potential targets, the energy benefits derived from their hunting and feeding as a cohesive group leave the dogs much better off in terms of a well-fed lifestyle than was previously thought.

Are wild dogs hyenas or dogs?

Neither, although they do belong to the same family (Canidae) as dogs, jackals and wolves.

When African wild dogs were first described by Coenraad Temminck, a Dutch zoologist and explorer in 1820, he reckoned that they were a type of hyena. So, he named them *Hyena picta* – the painted hyena (*picta* means 'painted' in Latin). Nowadays, they're classified as the only living member of the genus *Lycaon*, and are called *Lycaon pictus*. Incidentally, this current name is not much better. Although we've kept the 'painted' bit in the epithet *pictus*, *Lycaon* refers to wolves. And wild dogs are not wolves!

In Greek mythology, Lycaon was the legendary King of Arcadia, who tried to trick Zeus, King of the Gods, into eating roasted human flesh. He wanted to see if Zeus was indeed all-knowing. But crafty Zeus didn't fall for this deception. Enraged, he punished Lycaon by turning him into a wolf.

Even today, we haven't really decided what to call wild dogs. Popular literature also refers to them as the ornate wolf, painted wolf, painted lycaon, painted hunting dog, Cape hunting dog, African hunting dog, spotted dog or the painted dog.

In spite of all these names, obvious physiological differences set wild dogs apart from both dogs and wolves. For example, wild dogs differ from dogs and wolves in that their teeth are specialised for a hyper-carnivorous diet, they have large, rounded ears and blotchy colouration, and they only have four toes on their front feet – they lack the dewclaw characteristic of dogs and wolves.

Wild dogs and wolves did have a common ancestor millions of years ago, but they've since followed different evolutionary pathways. The question of how long ago and exactly where wolves were first tamed and domesticated is still a matter of great debate among scientists. But what is clear, from DNA testing, is that dogs are not descendants of a modern wolf species, as is commonly believed. DNA analyses suggest that dogs and modern wolves are both descendants of a wolf-like ancestor that lived in Eurasia between 15 000 and 30 000 years ago.

Wild dogs cannot be domesticated. Unlike dogs or wolves, they're not likely to accept humans as 'pack leaders' and in spite of their common ancestry long ago, wild dogs are unable to breed with dogs or wolves.

ZEBRA

Are zebras white with black stripes or black with white stripes?

They are black with white stripes.

All zebras have a unique pattern of white-on-black (or brown) stripes – like fingerprints. No two are the same. However, what all zebras do have in common is their black skin. The entire hair coat (or pelage) grows from follicles in the skin. Every follicle contains melanocytes – cells that are responsible for producing the pigment melanin, resulting in the hair's dark colouration – but the melanocytes in the 'white stripe' follicles have all been deactivated (turned off). As a result, no colour is produced in these zones, leaving them white.

Another way of answering this question could be to look at the embryo of a zebra, which is uniformly dark in colour; light areas start occurring only later when the melanocytes are deactivated.

So there it is, in black and white.

Why do zebras have stripes?

Some say that zebras have stripes because they don't want to be spotted . . .

There is much debate over at least three possible theories for the evolutionary development of zebra stripes: as a deterrent for biting flies such as tsetse flies and horseflies; for thermoregulation – the black-and-white stripes create air currents over the skin that regulate body temperature; and as antipredator camouflage. Conclusive evidence for the first two theories (biting-fly deterrent and thermoregulation) is yet to emerge, and studies seem to show that the stripes have no role in camouflage.

The 'protection from predators' theory is the most commonly held belief. It is usually supported by a hackneyed explanation that goes something like this: 'The dazzling stripes in a herd of running zebras confuse lions, making it difficult for them to target a specific individual – almost like "bedazzlement" camouflage.'

This makes little sense. Firstly, stripes, spots or shapes on an animal's fur are usually associated with the colour of the vegetation or the ground in their environment. As zebras sport highly contrasting, conspicuous black-and-white colouration and tend to live on open plains rather than in thick bush where the stripes could somehow fulfil a role in camouflage, this statement is probably already debunked.

Secondly, zebras tend to run from danger rather than standing still to rely on their so-called 'camouflage' for protection.

Finally, zebras are a preferred prey item for lions – they catch and eat *a lot* of them . . . every day! Far too many, it may seem, for this 'confusion-through-bedazzlement' theory to hold any water. So, who is actually confused here?

Are zebras and wildebeest best buddies?

Not necessarily. Many species that share the same predators will herd with each other to protect themselves from detection. That's why you'll often see impalas, kudus, wildebeest, zebras and giraffes close to one another. In fact, zebras get far more protective benefit from associating with giraffes than they do from being with wildebeest. For zebras, giraffes are an altogether better alarm system because giraffes have such an elevated view over the surroundings, like a guard high up in a watchtower.

The problem is that giraffes do not issue warning calls or grunts, so the zebras have to keep a beady eye on them, constantly taking cues from their body posture and behaviour. In fact, zebras are so confident in the predator-detection abilities of giraffes that they devote only a third of the time to vigilance as when giraffes are not present, research shows. Zebras are particularly alert to the 'stock-still stare' exhibited by giraffe when all is not well. (This is also a good tip if you ever find yourself in a survival situation and at the mercy of the bush. Giraffes tend to stand still and stare at you. Should they shift their stare in a different direction, there's a good chance that you should be taking note of a potential danger lurking in that direction.)

Are zebra and wildebeest food buddies?

So, if giraffes are such good threat spotters, why don't zebras prefer to associate with giraffes rather than wildebeest? It's probably got to do with feeding preferences, as giraffes are browsers and zebras are grazers. By sticking with other grazers – such as wildebeest – zebras get a better handle on the location and availability of food.

Popular literature and commonly 'accepted' explanations usually state that there are two reasons why zebras and wildebeest co-herd. Firstly, zebras prefer to eat longer, tougher grass, which opens up access for wildebeest to shorter, more palatable grass. Secondly, zebras, I'm told, have much better eyesight than wildebeest, while wildebeest have a better sense of hearing than zebras. Jointly, these characteristics combine to enable increased vigilance against predators.

There's no doubt that zebras and wildebeest will associate with each other in mixed herds, often while grazing together on open savannas. When one considers the theory that zebras eat taller grasses, allowing wildebeest access to the shorter grasses, the explanation seems to suggest that the wildebeest would not be able to feed on shorter grass at that very moment if the zebras had not prepared the way for them. Naturally, this is not the case. While they do have different grass feeding preferences, this symbiotic grazing benefit would only be realised in the broader grassland ecology context, and over seasonal periods. Not as proposed, at that moment.

The idea that zebras are the eyes and wildebeest are the ears in their little partnership may be true, but bear in mind that both species, even when not associated with each other, rely primarily on their eyesight and hearing to detect predators. There's no concrete evidence that these senses are developed to a greater or lesser extent within these species, or to what extent that would be. Moreover, it's unlikely that these two species need to stick together because of the often-quoted shortfall in their sensory abilities.

What is more likely is that these plains species will group together, especially in open areas, simply to have many more ears and eyes to raise the alarm, thereby reducing their risk of becoming prey.

Part 2

BIRDS

ABOUT BIRDS: GENERAL

Can birds fly upside down?

No. A bird's wings are designed so that the flight feathers are able to rigidly lock up, overlapping one another in order to create a rigid, continuous surface that resists strong airflow from below, almost like the slats that make up a Venetian blind.

But it doesn't work the other way around. If the bird tried to fly upside down, the airflow would prevent the individual flight feathers from locking in position and instead they would rotate to the 'open' position, letting air through. There would be no lift . . . and the bird would fall out of the sky.

Remarkably, some geese actually put this 'no-lift' principle to good use. While in full flight, they swing their entire bodies – wings, legs and all – into an upside-down position. At the same time, they rotate their necks so that the head still remains the right side up. This manoeuvre is called 'whiffling'.

Goose flying in an upside-down position.
This manoeuvre is called 'whiffling'.

Since the lift aerodynamics are now inverted, the bird immediately drops out of the sky and plummets earthwards. But there's method in this madness: they specifically perform this stunt as a means of evading raptors or of rapidly losing height when a fast landing is called for.

Why do some birds hop while others run?

Generally, the preference for hopping or running is determined by the length of a bird's legs, where it likes to forage and how efficient it is at using its energy. Long-legged birds walk or run, short-legged birds hop, and many (like secretary birds) are perfectly capable of doing both.

It makes sense for smaller, lightweight birds that spend most of their time foraging in bushes or trees to be able to hop between branches and twigs – it's easier to hop than to fly in the tree. Besides, hopping uses less energy than flying. And when these birds are on the ground, they'll habitually retain their hopping habit. Each hop is the equivalent of taking several steps to cover the same distance.

Ground-dwelling birds tend to walk or run rather than hop. Longer legs make walking faster. Some can run at great speeds when having to evade predators. Even then, running is more energy efficient than flying. That's why you'll see guinea fowl or francolin beating a blistering escape on foot, puffs of dust in their wake, and taking to the air only as a last resort. Some smaller ground-based birds, such as wagtails, are also runners.

Wading birds that spend lots of time near waterbodies or on the seashore, such as plovers or sandpipers, have long, spindly legs that are totally unsuited for hopping in their watery environment. However, the smaller plovers have relatively short legs, with which they can outrun incoming waves while feeding at the water's edge.

How do chicks breathe when they are still inside the egg?

No animal can live without oxygen. Embryos that develop inside a female use the umbilical cord to piggyback on the mom's ability to breathe in oxygen, distribute it to body tissues via the bloodstream and remove the waste product carbon dioxide that forms in the process of metabolism.

But what if, like a developing chick inside an egg, you're not plumbed into your mother's life-support system? Trust nature to have a workaround . . .

The contents of an egg are surrounded by two membranes directly under the shell. The egg, when laid, is warm (around 40 °C) but it soon cools, which causes its contents to shrink slightly. As a result, the membranes pull apart and form a small air sac directly under the shell.

The embryonic chick grows a sac-like pouch, the allantois, which fuses with the membrane surrounding the chick and its yolk. In this way the chick's circulatory system becomes 'connected' with the outside world, using the membrane like an external lung. The shell of the egg has thousands of microscopic pores through which oxygen diffuses onto the membrane's surface and into the chick's blood. Gaseous waste in the form of carbon dioxide moves in the opposite direction, out of the egg.

Which bird travels furthest during migration?

An Arctic tern (*Sterna paradisaea*) can travel 60 000–80 000 km each year. Why? Because, like most of us, they're sun worshippers.

These long-haulers mostly breed in the Arctic Circle during summer. But when the days start getting shorter, heralding the onset of another dark, brutal Arctic winter, the birds head south. Their journey tracks the summer season all the way down towards the other side of our planet, eventually ending when they reach their destination, the Antarctic Circle.

The Earth's seasons come about because the planet revolves around the Sun on a tilted axis. When the northern hemisphere is tilted towards the Sun, that part of Earth gets more sun exposure, which means the days are longer and warmer. Because of the tilted axis, the southern hemisphere receives less direct sunlight during this time and experiences shorter, colder days. As the Earth travels on its orbit around the Sun, things gradually change, so that about six months later the tables are turned: now the southern hemisphere gets its time in the sun while the northern hemisphere gets less direct exposure.

It's always cold in the polar regions, though; temperatures don't vary dramatically. But what does differ a lot is the amount of daylight the polar regions receive during winter and summer. In winter, the Arctic and Antarctic are in almost total darkness, while in summer, they're in sunlight for almost 24 hours a day.

It's therefore safe to say that Arctic terns experience more daylight than any other animal on Earth in the course of their travels.

Surviving during the long, dark days of the icy Arctic winter would be hard. But by being in a perpetual summer, they're assured of light all year round by which to catch insects or fish. Besides, the calmer weather at sea during summer allows for easier flight. Clearly, it's more advantageous to take on an epic migration than to endure a bitter, sunless winter.

The terns leave their northern breeding grounds in colonies. Just before the migration is about to begin, the noisy colony becomes quiet – a silence that is called 'dread'. After dread, the entire colony takes to the air as one to begin their journey.

The birds fly different routes on their southbound and northbound journeys, and they don't fly in a straight line in either direction. One study, using tiny sensors attached to migrating birds, showed that their southern migration from Greenland and Iceland is a leisurely trip of about 90 days, with a stopover of three to four weeks along the way. (This particular route passed offshore Namibia and South Africa.) The return trip back north was hastier, though. It took only about 40 days, with the birds flying up to 600 km a day to cover almost 25 000 km in total!

Arctic terns can live for more than 30 years. At an estimated total travel distance of 60 000–80 000 km every year, this equates to over two million kilometres over their lifetime. That's about three trips to the moon and back again!

Why do some birds use spider webs when they build their nests?

The simple answer is that threads from a spider web are like elastic duct tape, and a great way to hold a nest together.

Sunbirds in particular will use a wide variety of materials – leaves, lichen and even feathers – when building their nests. Adding a spider web into the mix helps to hold all these fairly flimsy materials firmly in place, giving the nest its characteristic purse shape.

Spider web strands are a perfect natural binding material. A spider web is light, thin, sticky and stretchy. And, even better, it's strong. In fact, spider silk is five times stronger than high-grade steel. It's also abundant.

Another advantage of using this versatile material is that its elasticity allows the nest to expand to accommodate the growing chicks. After all, in time they'll grow to be a lot bigger than the eggs from which they hatched!

It's little wonder then that many bird species make a point of collecting spider webs to incorporate into their nests. Not only is the silk harvested from existing spider's webs, but it's also recycled from previous nests that still have usable silk. In fact, it's so coveted in the nest-building season that brazen acts of silk theft are not uncommon, with attempts to steal it from other birds' active building sites.

Can birds smell?

Yes, they can. Until around 20 years ago, though, scientists were firmly under the impression that except for in a handful of species, birds generally did not have a sense of smell, or at least if they did, it was such an underdeveloped sense that it was considered insignificant. (The sense of smell is called olfaction.)

But new research proves otherwise – and it's interesting to understand why it's taken scientists so long to explore the mystery of bird olfaction. Somehow, birds have just been taken to rely almost entirely on their remarkably well-developed senses of vision and hearing for survival – so much so that it was always presumed that birds evolutionarily sacrificed their olfactory ability.

Yet some birds were known to be able to smell. Kiwis, for example, have nostrils on the tip of their beaks, which they use to sniff out worms and other invertebrate critters hiding in leaf litter. Turkey vultures will home in on the scent of carrion. Tube-nosed seabirds such as petrels and albatrosses also find food at sea using scent.

Just over a decade ago, it was discovered that in some migratory birds (for example, shearwaters), smell may be even more important than magnetic fields in helping them stay on track over vast distances.

Researchers at the Konrad Lorenz Institute in Vienna have shown that the black-legged kittiwake (a kind of seagull) selects a potential mate by determining its 'relatedness' through its odour: closer relatives have a more similar smell than unrelated individuals, a selection method seemingly more important than considering the size, colour or behaviour of their would-be mates, as was commonly believed. Penguins can also smell prey or sniff out their mates in crowded colonies. Some tits and starlings in Europe will travel considerable distances to collect very specific aromatic plants such as mint and lavender with which to line their nests. The aromatics are disinfectants that provide a sterile environment for developing chicks, improving their chances of survival.

We're only just starting to uncover the extent to which birds rely on smell for survival. But what scientists do know now is that birds use their sense of smell a lot more than was previously thought, even if it's not as developed as in other vertebrates.

Watch this space: I'm convinced that many more star(t)ling revelations are to come.

What should you do if you find a chick outside its nest?

I remember being taught as a child never to touch a chick while it's in the nest, because it would lead to the parents immediately rejecting the chick, cruelly kicking it out of the nest to die a lingering death. Many a bird lover wanting to put a chick back into the nest it obviously tumbled from has been caught between the devil and the deep blue sea like this. (I know of someone who cunningly used braai tongs to resettle an evacuee, lest she fatally condemn the chick with her 'scent of death'.)

It's not in our nature to simply look the other way when we find a helpless baby bird that (we believe) will most certainly perish without our intervention. But will it? Perhaps it wasn't pushed . . . perhaps it jumped?

So, here's what to do when you find yourself in this delicate situation. First determine whether the baby is a nestling or a fledgling.

Nestlings are very young, featherless bird, often with their eyes still closed, and they are almost completely helpless. They still need their parents to take care of them and may well have fallen out of the nest by accident. In such a case, there's no issue at all with briefly handling the youngster to put it back in its home (provided you know where the nest is). The parents won't abandon it if you've done so. I can't think of a good reason why they would, especially when one considers the strength of parental bonds in nature and the astonishing measures to which creatures will go to protect and care for their young. And besides, there's scant evidence that all birds recognise their young by their smell (see the previous entry on sense of smell in birds).

The case of fledglings may be different, though. Fledglings are more developed – the body is covered in feathers, they have a stubby tail and they will often react to a human's close presence. If you've found a fledgling, it could be that you happened upon it shortly after it left the nest on its maiden flight. The last thing it needs is to be put back into the nest – it will simply bail out again! And besides, it may still be under the watchful eyes and in the care of its parents, and you might just not see them close by.

So, in a nutshell: you can put the ugly, almost featherless nestlings back, but leave the endearing little 'cuties' alone, not because of their parents' reaction, but because they're at a different stage of their life journey. Even if we humans are concerned about cats, the cold, rain, cars and other dangers that could put a fledgling at risk, it's best to simply move the youngster to a safe area, where nature can resume its course. If it's been wounded or injured, or appears to be sick (immobile or falling over), special attention is the preferred option – a rescue that is best left to the experts.

AFRICAN DARTERS

How do African darters catch fish?

I'm fortunate enough to see an African darter (*Anhinga rufa*, also known as the snake bird) that regularly fishes in the tilapia-filled pond at my home, and I've always been intrigued by how it uses its bill to spear a fish with so much precision. Tilapia, in particular, are skittish, acutely attuned to any movement, and can dash away underwater in blinding bursts of speed, erupting into streaks and swirls of evasive action.

If its takeoff is anything to judge by, the bird seems somewhat ungainly. Surely it's an unequal contest between predator and prey?

A darter is a powerful swimmer, with large, webbed feet set far back under its body. But fast swimming alone will not get it its next meal – too much exaggerated movement will certainly spook the fish. And besides, there's no chance of the bird outswimming a fish.

To impale its piscatorial prey, the darter relies on stealth, coupled with the breakneck speed of its pecking action. This is thanks to a specialised hinge joint between the eighth and ninth vertebrae (this is responsible for the 'kink' you may see in the bird's neck when it's at rest). The joint has an array of powerful muscles and specialised vertebral attachments to rocket the bill forward with explosive speed. (Herons also use this mechanism.)

But let's just take a step back first. How does it actually get close enough to a fish? The answer lies in a combination of neutral buoyancy, which means it does not need to constantly fight either sinking to the bottom or bobbing to the surface, and efficient oxygen use, which allows the bird to remain underwater for up to a minute.

Neutral buoyancy is achieved, firstly, by completely saturating the feathers with water: no air bubbles are trapped between or under the feathers (unlike ducks and geese, which trap air between their waxy feathers and skin to help them stay afloat). Secondly, the darter's bones are denser than other birds', providing a ballast component. Thirdly, its air sacs are fairly small. These three things combined allow the darter to ride low in the water, with only the head and neck visible – like an avian submarine fitted with a periscope.

To get within range of its prey, the bird either swims really slowly or keeps almost dead still underwater, as if lying in ambush, waiting for an unsuspecting fish to venture within striking distance. To tip the scales in its favour and improve its chances in the shallows, it will even spread its wings slightly to create a shade canopy that will lure fish closer (the black heron also does this).

When a fish is close enough, the darter strikes at it side-on, with its bill slightly parted. The bill tip has backward-pointing, serrated edges, which act as barbs to help secure the skewered fish on the 'spear'.

But this presents some problems, as darters need to swallow their fishy bites head first. So the bird shakes the fish free of its barbed bill, tosses it into the air and catches it again – with the utmost precision (although it's not uncommon for the odd fish to be lost during this fiddly manoeuvre). The release-and-catch manoeuvre is no mean feat while you're bobbing along on an unstable watery surface.

I applaud every time.

Do African darters sun themselves to dry their feathers?

Indeed they do. But this is not the primary reason why they're seen sitting on sandbanks like sun-worshippers, with their wings and tails stretched out.

As their bodies are constantly submerged while in the water, with their feathers thoroughly saturated and wet to the skin, they lose a lot of heat. That's why their hunting excursions usually don't last for more than about 30 minutes at a time.

When they get out of the water, they perch on the bank, turn their back to face the sun and spread their wings and tail to dry. More importantly, though, is that the feathers on their backs are fluffed out and raised, allowing the warmth of the sun to fall directly onto the skin on their backs.

BEARDED VULTURES

Do bearded vultures feed on bones?

It's their preferred meal, yes. And they're the only animal in the world that feeds almost exclusively on bone – with a specific love of bone marrow, too.

Although their numbers are dwindling drastically worldwide,

bearded vultures (*Gypaetus barbatus*) are still found in isolated populations from China through Europe and to South Africa. They're
listed as near threatened by the International Union for Conservation
of Nature, but in South Africa many consider them critically endangered seeing that there are possibly only 100 breeding pairs left in the
Maloti–Drakensberg Mountains.

Adults weigh in at around 6 kg and they have a wingspan of 2.6 m.
Their red eyes, striking plumage and broad, diamond-shaped tails make
them impressive birds. Bearded vultures were given their name because
of their handsome black facemask with beard-like feathers protruding
from the chin. No bald heads here, like the other vultures . . . In fact,
the isiZulu name is *ukhozilwentshebe*, meaning 'eagle with a beard'.
The Afrikaans name – *baardaasvoël* – also refers to it as a vulture with
a beard. The other well-known name is lammergeier, from the German
word meaning 'lamb vulture'. In Germany, it was historically believed
that these birds not only attacked lambs, but also young children! Consequently, they were hated, feared and hunted to the extent that they
were eventually eradicated in the Alps.

Back to them bones. Bearded vultures are carrion feeders like the
rest of their kin. But what sets them apart from the rest is that they
feed mostly on a diet of bones and bone marrow.

Once other vultures have cleaned a carcass, bearded vultures swoop
in and use their sharp beaks to cut the bones free from the ligaments
and flesh attaching them to the skeleton. Smaller bones (around 25 cm
in length) are swallowed in one gulp. The bigger bones, those too large
to swallow, are broken up into smaller pieces – with some effort.

They grasp the bone in their talons and then fly up to a height of
up to 150 m, from where they drop the bone accurately onto the rocks
below. This action may need to be repeated several times before the
bone breaks. When it does break, the bird immediately glides or spirals
down to eat the manageable pieces, starting by licking out any exposed
bone marrow with a rough, scoop-like tongue. (There's about 15%
more energy in bone marrow than in meat, but I'd not be surprised if
all the effort that goes into smashing the bones far exceeds the energy
gain of 15%.)

Its strong gastric fluids easily digest bone, so the bird is ensured of a nutritious food source for which there is minimal competition. Perfect!

Live prey such as hares and hyraxes may also be seized on the wing, carried skywards and dropped in flight. Tortoises, especially, are unceremoniously dropped from up high onto rocks in order to smash open their shells.

In fact, Aeschylus – the playwright and father of Greek tragedy – was supposedly killed by a bearded vulture that dropped a tortoise on his head. The story goes that the bird mistook Aeschylus's bald head for the perfect rock upon which to drop its shell-shocked tortoise. A tragedy if ever there was one!

BEE-EATERS

Do bee-eaters get stung by bees?

Sometimes, but they learn quickly!

With their long, tweezer-like bills and aerodynamic wings and tails that allow for remarkable accuracy and agility in flight, bee-eaters catch flying insects on the wing, seldom hunting on the ground. But they don't hunt only bees; they'll also catch wasps, dragonflies, damselflies, butterflies and flies.

Small prey may be eaten at the moment in which they are caught, in the air, but when a larger insect is caught, the bee-eater returns to its perch to bash or rub its catch against the perch. This not only kills the insect before it is swallowed, but also helps to remove the stingers of stinging insects. It seems that this behaviour is genetically hard-wired in bee-eaters, as even youngsters do it when they first start hunting.

There are nine species of bee-eater commonly found in South Africa. Their closest relatives are rollers, hoopoes and kingfishers. In fact, when insects hatch in water, carmine bee-eaters mimic their kingfisher cousins by splashing directly into the water to capture insect larvae.

Beekeepers and bee-eaters have been embroiled in a long-standing feud, as especially rural honey farmers believe that the birds negatively affect honey production by feeding on the bees and decimating the hive populations. But studies have shown that this is not the case.

FAMILIAR CHATS

What makes a *spekvreter* such a familiar chap?

The story goes like this: during the Voortrekker days, when the Boers were forging into the (unfamiliar) interior of South Africa with their ox wagons, they constantly needed lubrication for the wagon wheels' hubs. Fat rendered from animals was a good way to keep the wheels well-oiled on the gruelling journeys, which often lasted for years.

For easy and frequent access on the long trek, this grease was stored in a wooden barrel or an iron pot hanging from the back of the wagon. It didn't take a little bird long to discover that the fat was much to its liking. Hence the Afrikaans name *spekvreter*, literally meaning 'fat eater'.

Over the years, these birds began to associate the wagons with food, alighting on the wheel hubs for a snack when the wagons stopped. When the intrepid explorers gradually established farms, the wagons stood semi-retired, not far from the homesteads.

But the association between wagon and bird remained, and the little birds soon became familiar residents around the homesteads, hence their English name: the familiar chat. The scientific name is *Cercomela familiaris*.

FLAMINGOS

Why are flamingos pink?

The name 'flamingo' is derived from the Spanish word *flamengo*, meaning 'flame-coloured'. Found in the Americas, southern Europe, Asia and Africa, these graceful, long-legged waders are renowned for their striking colouration, which varies from white or pinkish to almost scarlet red.

But unlike the genetically determined colouration of most other bird species, their pink hues are due to their food intake, not genetics. Flamingos are the personification of the phrase 'you are what you eat'!

Flamingos are filter feeders, using their beaks to strain out small crustaceans, molluscs, insects, larvae and different types of algae from the water in which they feed. The algae contain nutrients and natural dyes called carotenoids, particularly beta carotene (an orange-red pigment that's also found in vegetables such as tomatoes, pumpkin, sweet potato, spinach and, of course, carrots).

Carotenoids from the food get absorbed into a flamingo's system and end up in the skin and feathers, making the bird appear pink or red. The more of the pigment there is in its diet (which depends to a large extent on the proportion of algae that its watery broth contains relative to all the other foodstuffs, such as crustaceans and molluscs), the darker the bird's colour.

Algal concentrations, and thus also those of carotenoids, vary from place to place. That's why flamingos in different regions of the world are different shades of pink. Caribbean flamingos, for example, are spectacularly bright red to orange. On the other side of the spectrum are flamingos that occur in dryer regions (such as South Africa), which are not as brightly coloured owing to the lower concentration of carotenoids in their diet.

If a flamingo's food contains no carotenoids, new feathers will be pale and pink feathers will gradually moult away, eventually leaving the bird all white. Interestingly, flamingo chicks are dull grey to whitish, and their pink colouration starts to develop only from when they're about two years old.

There are six species of flamingo worldwide. Two of them, the greater flamingo (*Phoenicopterus roseus*) and the lesser flamingo (*Phoenicopterus minor*), the smallest type of flamingo, occur widely in southern Africa, except in extremely arid regions.

What's up with the one-legged stance?

Is it to conserve heat? To have less exposure to caustic water or waterborne parasites? Is it to help keep their feet dry? Maybe to reduce muscle fatigue so that they can respond more quickly when threatened by predators? These are some of the theories, but nobody knows for sure.

The most widely accepted explanation, though, is that standing on one leg gives them 'perfect balance with little effort'. Standing on two legs, like humans do, requires an animal to make tiny muscular adjustments all the time in order to maintain its balance. For flamingos everything changes when they lift up one leg: they become almost perfectly stable.

It's all in the design of the legs and how they attach to the body. (By the way, when you watch a flamingo walking, the bendy bit that you see is not the knee, but rather the ankle. The knee is much higher up, hidden within the bird's feathers.)

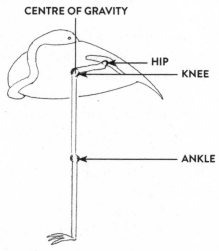

A flamingo's centre of gravity.

Researchers have found that when a flamingo lifts up its leg, the body mass shifts forward to become centred directly above the single foot instead of the feet being in line with the hips, as when the bird is standing on two feet. All the joints, ligaments and tendons in the supporting leg simply 'lock' into a rigid, stable position that requires minimal muscular effort to keep the bird upright and perfectly balanced, even when sleeping.

In fact, in the study in which scientists investigated the physics of the one-legged stance, they found that they could even pose a dead flamingo on one leg and it would remain standing there, upright and perfectly balanced.

So, that's *how* flamingos are able to stand on one leg. But exactly *why* they do it still remains unanswered, especially as they don't constantly stand on one leg while resting. If this were such an important energy-saving mechanism, would they then not do it all the time? The jury is still out.

GREEN-BACKED HERONS

Does the green-backed heron use bait to catch fish?

Yes, the green-backed (striated) heron, *Butorides striata*, is one of the few birds in the world known to use bait to capture its prey.

When I was a presenter on 'VeldFocus', an insert on the nature programme *50/50* on TV, I received several videos from viewers showing these birds luring fish within striking distance using bait. The bait that these resourceful birds use includes insects, feathers and even pieces of bread discarded by fishermen.

Green-backed herons are known to use bait to catch fish.

Using their bills, they pick up suitable bait on the shore and then carry it to the water, where it is carefully placed to float on the surface. The bird then waits patiently, keeping dead still, with the tip of its bill hovering right at that spot. Should a fish investigate the bait, the heron is perfectly positioned to lunge, grab and swallow it.

HAMERKOPS

Why are hamerkop nests so big?

Hamerkop nests are not easily missed – they can be up to 2 m wide and as high, and are usually seen in large trees or on cliff ledges. There's no definitive answer as to why these birds create such big nests, but the most accepted theory is that their size could serve as a territorial marker.

The nests are built of sticks, twigs, leaves and grass. A single entrance towards the bottom of the nest is lined with mud, as is the breeding chamber inside, around which the impenetrable fortress is meticulously constructed. Contrary to belief, a breeding pair does not necessarily keep using the nest for years on end. Despite putting huge effort into constructing a nest, hamerkops are compulsive builders, and they may abandon one nest to build another in the same year. Alternatively, the birds may stay put for several years and dutifully add to their home over time.

These enormous structures do not go unnoticed by other species. Owls have been known to build their nests on top of hamerkops', while smaller bird species and tree-nesting geese and ducks attach their nests to the main structure. Snakes and monitor lizards, genets, tree squirrels, mongooses and even bees find these stick citadels useful for breeding, hunting, refuge or residence. Naturally, if any of the squatters pose a threat to the hamerkop pair, they abandon the nest and immediately begin the gargantuan task of constructing another.

The impressive nest size may also be the reason why the hamerkop is revered in some African cultures. The Zulu (who call it *uthekwane*) believe that their home will be destroyed by fire if the nest is tampered with. The Kalahari San call it the 'lightning bird', believing that those who rob the nest of its eggs will be struck by lightning. In contrast, some African tribes perceive the birds as inept, clumsy frog hunters while others deem them notoriously dim-witted. Who knows why, but say what you like, they're high profile . . .

HONEYGUIDES

Do these birds lead humans to honey?

Yes. Engaging stories of the symbiotic relationship between honey-guides and humans are as comforting as they are satisfying – a fairytale relationship in which people and nature work together in harmony.

Unable to get the hive open on its own, the bird exhorts a human to assist it with its tweets and by fluttering from tree to tree, dutifully guiding its human helper to the treasure. The human then breaks open the hive, extracts the honey and leaves a morsel in appreciation for the selfless honeyguide.

Contrary to belief, though, the bird is not after the honey, but rather the wax, bees, and pupae and larvae inside the hive. Honeyguides are thought to be the only birds that can digest beeswax.

But humans use the relationship, too, for they may be as eager to get to a hive as the birds – although for the honey rather than the wax. In parts of Africa, wild honeyguides have learned to listen for specific human calls to team up with a fellow hive hunter, and so both parties increase their hit rate. It's a remarkable relationship, with one partner knowing where the hive is, while the other has the strength, smoke and tools to access it.

Do the birds lead honey badgers to a hive?

No. Contrary to what is widely known as 'fact', there exists no compelling evidence that honeyguides and honey badgers (called *ratels* in Afrikaans) have a mutualistic relationship. In fact, research has shown that honey badgers don't respond to the birds' calls at all.

This is in spite of the assumed relationship often being chronicled, even in David Attenborough's *The Life of Birds*, YouTube videos and personal observations. (There's even a video hoax that was made with a stuffed honeyguide and a tame badger!) The misconception may be based simply on both animals having 'honey' as the first part of their name, although the birds prefer wax over honey (see previous entry). Honey badgers, though, will eat almost anything, including honey.

I have no doubt that there have been occasions when, fortuitously, a honeyguide may have tried to elicit a response from a honey badger; they've done it with other animals, like baboons and mongooses. But the bird's overtures would have been met with little response. Besides, honey badgers aren't the best choice for a partner in hive hunting: they're mostly nocturnal, don't climb trees very well (not that hives are necessarily in trees) and don't see or hear that well.

Are honeyguide chicks brutal killers?

Greater honeyguides take extreme measures to ensure the survival of their offspring – and employ brutal, even terrifying, techniques.

Adult females are brood parasites, meaning that they will lay their eggs in the nests of other birds, like cuckoos. This deceitfully tricks the host birds into incubating the imposter egg and raising the chick as their own.

When a honeyguide is ready to lay, the first objective is to find a suitable nest. The obvious choice is a nest that already has eggs in it, laid by the rightful owner. But this could mean that when the honeyguide's egg hatches, it will need to compete with the host's chicks for food.

To ensure that her chick will get undivided attention and resources when it hatches, the honeyguide mom pitilessly punctures the host's eggs, extinguishing any chance of competition.

But what if she doesn't succeed in sabotaging every host egg and a competing hatchling survives? Or if the host lays more eggs *after* the honeyguide has laid hers?

That's where the honeyguide hatchling steps into the breach and mops up. Far from being helpless, inarticulate and clumsy, as we often think of chicks, the youngster is armed with a lethal spike at the tip of its bill. Despite being featherless and blind, the chick will kill any other contenders unfortunate enough to find themselves in the same nest within minutes of hatching, slashing viciously and repeatedly with its deadly stiletto-tipped bill. (If it were a horror movie, this is where the screaming would start . . .)

A honeyguide chick thus leaves a nest only after the foster mom's offspring have all been successfully killed. Yet this is the bird destined to be loved and revered by humans for selflessly guiding them to honey. Yin and yang.

Honeyguide hatchling showing its lethal bill hooks.

HORNBILLS

Why does a female lock herself up in her nest after mating?

Red-, grey- and yellow-billed hornbills have remarkable nesting habits, based on a relationship that requires a pair's total dependence on each other.

In summer, males search for a partner using their distinctive display: wings out, head down and calling. Pairs are monogamous, but only for one season.

After mating, a suitable hole is identified in a tree, which the female will enter. She then goes into a moult, shedding all her tail and flight feathers (darkness possibly activates a hormonal trigger for this). The male brings her mud and plant material, which she may also mix with faecal matter, to make a kind of 'cement' that she uses to completely seal off the hole, bar a narrow vertical slit through which the male can feed her. By imprisoning herself like this, she protects herself and her eggs from predators or other hole-nesting birds. The male also brings her material with which to line the nest, and feeds her regurgitated food or insects that he has captured.

The female and chicks also defecate through the slit, ejecting their faecal matter forcefully away from the nest.

During her imprisonment in the chamber, the female is entirely reliant on her partner for survival. Should he shirk his responsibilities, or if anything happens to him, she may die.

She lays between three and five eggs, beginning to incubate them as soon as the first one has been laid, and the eggs hatch from around 25 days later. The male's workload now increases considerably, as he needs to feed the female *and* the chicks.

By this time the female's flight feathers have started growing back. About two weeks after the chicks have hatched, the female breaks free from her cell. It's probably an issue of space, as it gets crowded inside the nest. The chicks all keep their tail feathers upright and continue to defecate forcefully through the opening (as they did while their mother was still there). Using new material, the entire family is now involved in resealing the nest: the adults working from the outside, the chicks from the inside. Both adults now feed the chicks through the narrow slit. Around three weeks after the female broke out, the youngsters begin to break the nest, their flight feathers now having developed. They stick around for about three more weeks, foraging with the adults, before moving off on their own.

The breeding pair may use the same nest for years.

KINGFISHERS

Why does a kingfisher bash its prey?

Contrary to popular belief, it's not to tenderise its catch. After all, since it swallows its prey whole, the bird is not faced with the daunting prospect of chewing it with blunt teeth, and therefore there would be no point in tenderising it first.

'Kingfisher' is a misleading name for this bird family, as not all species catch fish. Of the ten kingfisher species in southern Africa, six frequent well-wooded areas in search of their prey, with only a few of them primarily hunting fish. And those that do fish may also catch scorpions, reptiles, rodents, birds, frogs, crustaceans and insects, like their woodland kin.

Repeatedly bashing its prey (whether it's a fish or something else) against its perch by vigorously swinging its head from side to side, the bird presumably stuns the fish to the point of immobility. It's also easier to manoeuvre a 'stunned' fish into a head-first swallowing position by using only a few deft flicks of the bill. This is essential to prevent fins, scales and spines from catching in the bird's throat – swallowing a violently struggling fish armoured with sharp spines is bound to end badly . . .

OSTRICHES

Do ostriches hide their heads in the sand?

No, it's a myth – one that's so well entrenched in our minds that it's even used as a powerful metaphor to describe someone who wilfully ignores, or foolishly refuses, to acknowledge a situation.

This myth likely originated from the writings of Pliny the Elder (23–79 CE), a Roman author, naturalist and philosopher with an unmatched curiosity for all things. He studied and wrote tirelessly in an astonishing quest to document all the knowledge within the Roman Empire at the time. His observations were revered and endured as a principal source of knowledge throughout the Dark Ages.

It was Pliny who wrote about ostriches in his Natural History encyclopaedia almost 2 000 years ago. But he got it wrong (although it was an error with consequences that were maybe not quite as disastrous as his ill-fated rush to Pompeii when Vesuvius erupted in 79 CE . . .)

Of ostriches Pliny wrote (may I say unwisely?) that 'their stupidity is no less remarkable, for although the rest of their body is so large, they imagine, when they have thrust their head and neck into a bush, that the whole of the body is concealed'.

The incorrect assumption that ostriches stick their heads in the sand – to hide from predators, I've heard – probably stems from here, or perhaps even from observations that the head is often down and cannot be seen while the bird is feeding, turning its eggs or on the nest, trying to conceal itself by lowering its 'periscope'.

Although ostriches are thought to be on the lower rungs of the bird intelligence ladder, even their birdbrain reasoning ability can't be so poor that they would bury their reputation with such a foolhardy action . . .

OWLS

Why is a group of owls called a parliament?

Is it because they're deemed to be wise, as many Western cultures believe? The reason is far less philosophical, it seems.

The usage probably derives from literature. C.S. Lewis was the first to use the term in his 1950s children's classic, *The Chronicles of Narnia*, to describe a council of owls meeting at night to deliberate the affairs of Narnia, and it has since become entrenched in English usage.

It seems Lewis adapted the term from a poem written by Geoffrey Chaucer (of *Canterbury Tales* fame) some 600 years earlier with the title (in modern English) 'Parliament of Fowls'. The poem describes all the Earth's birds meeting on St Valentine's Day to choose their mates – a matter indeed worthy of much deliberation.

Do ear tufts help owls to camouflage themselves?

Many people will tell you that when at rest, some owls sit dead still and erect the pointy tufts of feathers at the top of their heads to make themselves 'disappear' from view in a tree. The popular reasoning goes that these tufts look like mammal ears and so break up their body outline, and also mimic twigs, sticks, bark or lichen, which makes for good camouflage. In this way they can protect themselves from predators and avoid being subjected to sustained mobbing by smaller bird species. (Mobbing is a cooperative attacking or harassing, anti-predatory behaviour that not only alerts other birds to the presence of the owl, but is also an attempt to drive the unwelcome intruder away.)

But the reasoning makes little sense. How would owl predators or other birds, over millions of years of co-existence, not have cottoned on to the 'tuft' trick? Clearly, some have; it's certainly not uncommon to see owls (with tufted 'ears' no less) being thoroughly mobbed. In fact, the incessant mobbing of roosting owls is often a dead giveaway to their precise location.

Moreover, not all owls have ear tufts. Only 50 of the world's 132 species have them (of the 12 species of owl in our subregion, only 6), which suggests that ear tufts may not be all that essential for camouflage.

As for the idea that the tufts break up the outline of an owl's body, it's only the head really, around a third of the of the body, that marginally experiences a shape change through the erection of ear tufts. I can't help imagining a conceited Verreaux's eagle-owl (*Ketupa lacteus*) pretending to be a giant piece of lichen, confidently upping and downing its ear tufts while muttering, 'Now you see me, now you don't.'

Lastly, I'm not convinced that using feathery tufts on your head to pretend that you have mammal-like ears will dissuade, scare or repel predatory mammals. If anything, a mammal-like face could attract other predators.

For now, we simply don't know. Perhaps it's something a parliament (of owls) should debate?

What makes owls such good night-time hunters?

When it comes to birds hunting prey, owls take over the night shift from their day-shift cousins, raptors such as hawks, buzzards and eagles. Consequently, they've evolved a suite of remarkable adaptations to fully exploit their nocturnal way of life: acute night vision, facial discs, enhanced hearing, silent flight and vascular adaptations to allow their heads to rotate.

Owls have characteristically large, forward-facing eyes. So large are they that the eyes occupy most of the skull cavity (leaving little room for a brain). The eyes are fixed in place, with no muscles to allow the eyes to move when the head is held still (this is different from how mammals' eyes move, including ours). But owls have fixed this by being able to turn their entire head 270 degrees, whether from left to right or right to left. (We can turn our heads only about 90 degrees to either side from the front.)

Coupled with the ability to see right around their bodies, owls also have eyes that are perfectly adapted to night vision. However, it's a myth to say that they can see in total darkness – no animal can. Eyes can function only in the presence of light, even if it is a marginal amount. The structure of owl eyes includes a tapetum lucidum, a reflective layer behind the retina that enhances visibility under low light conditions. Many nocturnal animals' eyes have this adaptation, which is what causes the characteristic 'eye shine' reflected in head-lamps at night.

Owls also rely on sensitive hearing to help them hunt at night (and it's got nothing to do with their ear tufts!). The disc on an owl's face acts like a satellite dish to capture and channel sound to the owl's ears, which look like slits on either side of the skull under the feathers on the head, and lead to a large ear canal. The shape of the disc can be altered by special muscles that control the stiff disc feathers. In some species the ears are asymmetrical, meaning that one ear is situated higher than the other on either side of the skull. This allows for enhanced hearing because they can 'tune in' to both the vertical and the horizontal axes, pinpointing precisely where a sound is coming from.

Their feathers and wings are also adapted to their stealth night life. Large wings and a light body enable them to fly without much effort. Instead of having to flap to stay in the air, the large wings allow them to glide silently. In addition, several adaptations to the feathers absorb turbulence and muffle sound, ensuring almost soundless flight.

Why do owls bob their heads?

All the better to focus on a target. Not only do they bob their heads curiously from side to side, up and down or forward and back, but they also sometimes weave and gyrate their entire body rhythmically in a comical, dancing motion at the same time.

Since their eyes are fixed in their heads and unable to move (see an earlier entry), the entire head needs to be moved for the bird to get different perspectives on an object. The animated head movements are therefore a way of 'triangulating' the object or prey, so that its exact position and distance can be determined.

OXPECKERS

Are red and yellow bills the only difference between oxpecker species?

There are two species of oxpecker, namely the red-billed oxpecker (*Buphagus erythrorynchus*) and the yellow-billed oxpecker (*Buphagus africanus*). But the names suggest a somewhat exaggerated difference in their appearance: only the *base* of the yellow-billed bird's bill is yellow; the front half is red.

The yellow-billed oxpecker has a has a comparatively heavier bill than its red-billed cousin and it's a slightly bigger bird with a beige rump. To make matters a bit more confusing, red-bills have a yellow ring around the eye, absent in the yellow-billed bird.

The yellow-billed oxpecker is scarce. By the early 1900s, these birds had become virtually extinct in South Africa because of threats such as toxic cattle dips and the rinderpest. But in 1979 they miraculously reappeared in the northern Kruger Park, and have since spread throughout the park and into neighbouring areas.

Some people believe that you can spot a yellow-billed oxpecker only in the northern regions of the park, but they've been seen towards the southern boundaries too. Look out for them – a creature that's thwarted the threat of extinction is always a special sighting.

Are these birds friend or foe to their hosts?

There is some controversy about whether oxpeckers are benevolent tick eaters or malevolent, bloodthirsty vampires.

Oxpeckers rid their hosts of ectoparasites, which surely makes them valuable allies. But it's also been noted that these birds pick at and open up wounds in their quest to obtain a blood meal. This impedes the healing process and may even exacerbate the injury, as the wounds persist and are further exposed to possible infection. That would put them firmly in the enemy camp.

So, where's the middle road on this one? Is the oxpecker in a mutually beneficial relationship with its host or is it just an opportunistic parasite?

Here's how we can make sense of it. Oxpeckers will hoover up almost anything that they're able to extract from the surface of an animal. It's a veritable smorgasbord: ticks, biting flies, open wounds, maggots, dead skin, scabs, saliva, mucus, blood. Oh, and earwax! To top this off, they also pluck fur from their hosts, which they use to line their nests.

No wonder the hosts often appear 'reluctantly tolerant' of their visits. In fact, elephants don't tolerate them at all, nor do some of the small antelope species.

But in the birds' favour, studies show that they primarily target larger herbivores, often favouring individuals with high ectoparasite loads; however, they don't specifically target animals with wounds. In fact, studies have shown that they much prefer (in more than 90% of cases) bugs over blood. Insects and other little invertebrate critters accumulate mainly around the eyes, ears, nose, mouth and anogenital regions of the host. Another advantage is that oxpeckers cause a commotion with loud, grating alarm calls when a predator approaches, and so act as an early-warning system that dutifully alerts their hosts to the impending threat.

Overall then, oxpeckers seem to do more good than harm.

 # SANDGROUSE

Can sandgrouse transport water in their feathers?

Sandgrouse (of which there are 16 species across the drier parts of Africa and Asia) are seed eaters and so need to drink regularly because they get very little water from their natural diets. This is a problem for hatchlings, who begin feeding on hard seeds almost immediately after they hatch, and so the chicks are therefore also obligate drinkers.

(Sandgrouse are the only birds in Africa, and among only a few in the world, whose chicks start feeding on hard food so soon.)

But sandgrouse dads get around this problem by soaking specially modified belly feathers to carry water to their chicks, which can be up to 30 km away. This is usually only done in the mornings, not in the evenings as is commonly believed.

The male bird flies to water and wades into the shallows. Here he starts a rocking motion in the water to thoroughly soak his belly feathers. Upon returning to the nest, he stands upright in front of the chicks, allowing them to 'strip' water from his sodden feathers by using their bills like tiny 'squeegees'.

The remarkable water-retaining ability of sandgrouse belly feathers is due to unique feather structures not found in other birds. When these feathers come into contact with water, delicate filaments on the ends of ribbon-like barbules project at right angles to the plane of the feather, allowing water to be trapped in this meshwork by interfacial tension and capillarity. In this way, the belly feathers can absorb about one-and-a-half tablespoons (22 ml) of water.

The belly feathers are also extremely robust and resist structural breakdown, despite repeated 'punishment' through wetting and drying, or daily stripping by the chicks, which need to be hydrated for up to eight weeks. The feathers don't fray or twist out of shape and retain their vital water-absorption abilities for as long as it takes.

SPOONBILLS

Are spoonbills spoonfed?

Indeed they are. Spoonbills have a long bill, flattened at the end to look almost like a wooden spoon. The top of the 'spoon' is curved, while the bottom is flat.

It is commonly believed that spoonbills feed simply by wading forward while sweeping the partially opened bill from side to side, snapping the sensitive bill shut when it comes into contact with a potential food item.

African spoonbill. The bill is uniquely adapted for feeding underwater.

Although this is not incorrect, there's a more complex mechanism at work. Because the spoonbill's beak has a curved top and flat bottom (resembling the shape of an aeroplane wing), it acts as a hydrofoil, creating 'lift' as the partially open bill is moved from side to side in the water. As a result of the sideways action, two streams of fluid are moving at different speeds (and pressures) relative to each other. The faster stream – over the curved surface – has less pressure because it needs to travel slightly further in the same time as the slower stream travels over the flat surface. The pressure difference causes a net upward force exerted on the flat surface (this is an application of Bernoulli's principle, which partially explains why aircraft achieve lift).

The upward 'lift' creates spirals over an area adjacent to the beak, which lifts or channels potential food items towards the open bill, ready to snap shut when they're detected.

So, spoonbills really do cause quite a stir when feeding . . .

SPUR-WINGED GEESE

Are their spurs and flesh poisonous?

No, it's a myth. That doesn't mean that you won't become infected if you're injured by such a spur, though . . . just as you may develop an infection from an injury from a tussle with any creature. In fact, I still bear a scar on my knee from a spur injury, inflicted on me by an angry goose when I was a child.

Spur-winged geese (*Plectropterus gambensis*) were given their name because of the stout, bony spine that projects formidably forward from the bend (wrist) in their wings. It's known as a carpal spur, and the males' spurs are bigger than those of the females.

Spur-winged goose. Note the bony spur on the bend of the wing.

These geese are known for being aggressive, especially during the breeding season. Males may violently attack one another, putting their spurs to good use against their opponents.

I've often been warned – sagely – that these spurs are venomous (even deadly). Not so. I must presume that this belief stems from the equally fearsome myth that the flesh of spur-winged geese is poisonous, as a defence against predators.

It's all become a rather muddled story, though. Spur-winged geese are widely distributed throughout sub-Saharan Africa. Although predominantly plant eaters, some populations in Gambia may also feed on poisonous blister beetles found in that country, the toxins of which are absorbed into their own tissues. The toxin is called cantharidin and as little as 10 mg can be fatal to humans. But this phenomenon is not known to occur here in South Africa.

Interestingly, one of the effects of cantharidin when ingested by humans is to cause swelling in the genitals. It's no surprise then that cantharidin has been used as an aphrodisiac for centuries. In fact, the love potion Spanish Fly originally contained cantharidin from blister beetles. The Romans also used it: they mixed dried blister beetle powder with sweet drinks to get things going. And many died – from inflammation rather than infatuation.

That's why it's said that eating the flesh of a spur-winged goose will kill you, and you're at equal risk if stabbed by the spurs.

In reality, though, I don't know of fatalities as a result of ingesting spur-winged goose flesh, most certainly not in South Africa. In fact, they're a firm favourite on the tables of some households in this neck of the woods.

SUNBIRDS

How do they feed?

Sunbirds – not to be confused with sugarbirds, hummingbirds or honeysuckle (which is a plant) – are specialist nectar feeders that perch gingerly on a flower stalk while feeding. (This is different from a hummingbird, which feeds exclusively while in the air, flapping its wings up to 80 times per second.)

The sugar-rich nectar is often deep within a flower and difficult to reach, unless you're specifically adapted to do so. The sunbird's long, narrow curved bill is a good start, but I've often wondered how exactly, once they've stuck their bill inside a tubular flower, do they take in nectar? Do they lick it up or suck it in?

A sunbird's tongue is a thin tube that can be longer than the bill itself. Once the bird inserts its bill in the flower, it pushes out its tongue and draws up the nectar as if through a straw.

Even though sunbirds specialise in feeding on nectar, that's not all they eat. They'll also feed on insects and spiders to supplement their diet. In fact, some sunbirds have beaks with serrated edges at the tip, all the better to grip insects with.

 # SWALLOWS

Why do swallows return to the same nests?

Wouldn't you want to come home too after a 10 000 km journey?

Most birds build a new nest every season in which to lay their eggs and raise their chicks. But swallows will usually return to the nest they used the previous year, and the year before that . . . Their well-constructed mud nests are known to have been used by different pairs for 10–15 years in succession. The concept of 'nest faithfulness' – when creatures habitually return to a particular area or place – is called philopatry.

Swallows build their nests using balls of mud that they gather meticulously from a suitable site and then plaster together with care to get the perfect size and shape for their nesting real estate. Research suggests it takes around 13 000 return trips to gather enough mud pellets for a typical nest – and that the female does three-quarters of the work, while the males (particularly those with longer tail feathers, apparently) take the easy way out and only swoop in for the last quarter of the job.

When swallows return after a migratory journey of about 10 000 km, it makes sense for a female to save whatever fat reserves are left in her body to support the formation of a clutch of eggs, rather than expending energy on building a nest.

The other advantage of reusing the same nest is that swallows will often attempt to squeeze in a second brood in a season. Staying put in the same home rather than building a new one saves a lot of energy and gives them nearly two weeks extra to breed.

However, nests are often taken over by other species, even while occupied by the swallows. House sparrows in particular are notorious in this sense, and are known to evict the rightful owners while destroying their eggs and chicks.

SWIFTS

Is it true that swifts never land because they cannot take off from the ground?

No. But there's more to it than that . . .

Swifts are hardly ever found on the ground because there's no need for them to be there. They're able to spend years in the sky, eating, drinking, sleeping and even mating on the wing. Young swifts that have left the nest may spend between three and four years just flying before starting to breed.

Their nests are built high up under bridges or eaves so that the birds are able to drop directly into flight from the nest entrance. Even the nesting material is airborne and gathered in flight: feathers, paper, bits of grass, leaves and seeds are mixed with saliva and incorporated into the nest structure.

Swifts drink by catching raindrops or flying low over water and skimming mouthfuls from the surface.

There's a common belief that if a swift is found on the ground, the only way to save its life is to hurl it back into the sky because it is unable to take off from the ground. Please never do that! The reason is simple: if the bird doesn't spread its wings and fly, you may be responsible for causing it grave injury as it comes crashing down again into the ground.

If you find any bird on the ground, first try to gently encourage it to take off by itself, without picking it up. In the case of a swift, it should be well able to launch itself into the air with its powerful wings, provided it has enough space to flap its way into flight.

If the grounded bird is not able to take off, pick it up gently and slowly move your outstretched arm up and down to encourage it to fly. Sadly, most birds that can't, or won't, take off from your hand are often too far gone to do so. The best thing to do then is to contact your local veterinarian or wildlife rehabilitation centre.

TURACOS

Colouration

The red and green colours we see on birds' bodies are often due to somewhat of a kaleidoscope effect, coming about as a result of light reflecting off the feather structures.

Not so in turacos, though. (These birds were formerly known as loeries in South Africa, but have been renamed in line with international conventions. The only exception is the former grey loerie, which is now called the grey go-away-bird.)

Turacos are unique in that they are the only birds known to produce true red and green colouration. The colours are produced by two different copper pigments in their feathers – turacoverdin for green feathers and turacin for the red flight feathers.

I've often heard that if you stir a glass of water with a red turaco feather, the water will turn a pale reddish colour too. It suggests that the feathers' colour would dissolve, run or fade in the rain – which is highly unlikely.

Contrary to common belief, Knysna turacos are not confined to the Knysna region. They have a wide distribution and are found in evergreen coastal forests from the Western Cape to Mpumalanga and Eswatini.

 # VULTURES

How come they arrive at a carcass so quickly and en masse?

They simply keep a beady eye on one another.

Vultures are known for their remarkably good eyesight. Soaring effortlessly on thermals, they can cover hundreds of kilometres each day in their quest to find a meal. But they're not only looking at the ground for food. More importantly, they're watching their soaring neighbours, widespread and far away, who, in turn, are watching *their* neighbours . . . and so on.

In this way, visual contact is maintained by large numbers of vultures at any time, each on their own mission, but collectively patrolling vast surface areas of tens of thousands of square kilometres. This inflight sweep of 'mile-high' flyers can sometimes span a few countries at a time. Down on the ground, we're blissfully unaware of them.

If one of the vultures spots a carcass, it will immediately drop into a purposeful and determined descent towards the target. Its watchful neighbours will immediately follow suit, homing in on the same point of descent. And their neighbours will follow, too. It's almost like they're diving down a funnel, of which the open end continues to widen like a ripple on a pond as the message spreads through the skies.

Arriving at the carcass on the ground, all from different directions and seemingly out of nowhere, they typically find that there's not enough to share, and then the squabbling begins . . .

WOODPECKERS

Do they get brain damage beating their heads against trees?
Imagine yourself repeatedly slamming your head into a solid wall, day in and day out, all your life.

That's what woodpeckers do – often against (im-peckably?) hard surfaces. The force it creates on their heads is said to be more than 10 times what would cause concussion in humans. So why don't their heads hurt?

Woodpeckers have developed a number of adaptations to prevent injury. Firstly, their bodies are designed to absorb much of the force experienced by the jarring blows, with the beak and skull directing most of the impact energy into the rest of the body.

They also retract their long tongue (which is sometimes up to three times the length of the beak) and wrap it around the back of the skull like a shock absorber, cushioning the brain against impact.

Woodpeckers have small brains that are packed very tightly into the skull. This means there's no space for the brain to move around on impact, which is typically the cause of concussion. A small brain also increases the surface area-to-weight ratio. As a result, less damage is caused because the impact force is absorbed over a relatively large area.

Lastly, the very strong bone in the woodpecker's skull is quite spongy, further helping to absorb any impact on the head.

Studies on woodpeckers' remarkable ability to protect themselves against brain injury from sudden impacts or vibrations may unlock biological mechanisms that can be used to develop protective headgear and helmets to help protect humans from severe head injuries during collisions.

REPTILES AND AMPHIBIANS

CHAMELEONS

How do chameleons change colour?

A chameleon's ability to change colour seems like magic. In fact, chameleons are often attributed with mystical powers because of this capacity. But their colour change is just biology: they do it by controlling how pigments inside their skin cells are distributed.

Chameleons have different layers of skin, each with specialised cells called chromatophores. Chromatophores in the different layers contain different pigments. Using nerve impulses and hormones, the chameleon controls how the pigments are distributed within the chromatophores.

When the pigments are spread throughout the cell, they reflect more light and so produce more colour. If the pigments are compacted in the centre of the cell, the cell appears transparent. Different colours and even different patterns are produced by changing the colour activity of the chromatophores.

Do chameleons change their colour to camouflage themselves?

No, it's a myth. The closest they get to 'camouflaging' themselves is that their default colouration – natural hues of greens or browns – happens to match the background colour of their typical surroundings.

Many people seem to think – mistakenly – that chameleons can change their colour to blend in perfectly with their background.

Just as we use language, birds use song and glow-worms use light to communicate, chameleons use colour. Studies have shown that a chameleon's colour tells other chameleons what mood they're in. The lighter the chameleon, the more tranquil and relaxed its mood; the darker or more intense, the more unsettled or angry the individual. This is important, especially if males want to signal their approachability

123

or intentions to females and to other male competitors – or predators.

Chameleons – like all reptiles – are cold-blooded animals, which means they rely on their environment to control their body temperature. Chameleons change their colour to help with this: when they become darker, they can absorb more heat, and when they change to a lighter hue, they will reflect more heat.

How does a chameleon catch prey with its tongue?

The chameleon's tongue is a remarkable thing, capable of shooting out and catching prey at an incredible speed. If it were a car, it would be able to accelerate from 0 km/h to 100 km/h in just a hundredth of a second. The fastest cars in the world, though, manage this in a tardy two seconds . . . How is such an astonishing feat possible?

A chameleon catching its prey.

Three things: the tongue is long – up to 1.5 times the length of the chameleon's body, it's attached to strong muscles and it's hollow. Because it's hollow it can be compressed tightly over a stiff, tapered cartilage spike (called the hyoid horn). The tongue itself is folded up, concertina style, over this bony structure, almost like when you push up the whole length of a long sleeve, squeezing it into a compressed bundle of fabric at the armpit. The hyoid tapers forward from its anchor inside the bottom of the throat (so, in the shirt sleeve example, towards your hand, with the armpit representing the bottom of the throat).

The combination of the compressed tongue, which is 'locked and loaded', and then over a tapered structure, and its position at the back of the throat makes for a highly effective weapon. When prey is sighted, the head is aimed at the target with precision. Then the entire assembly is moved forward and upward, ready to release, and the jaws open like a bomb bay.

Rings of muscle contract against the surface of the hyoid bone. Because the structure is tapered, the tongue is forced forward. It shoots off the tapered bone and out of the mouth at an incredible speed.

Because the contact surface between the muscles and the tapered bone is well lubricated, the tongue rockets off the bone like a ballistic, telescopic catapult. (It's a 'slip of the tongue' in the true sense!) You can think of it almost like squeezing a slippery pip from an orange, pressing hard between your fingers until the pip is suddenly ejected forward. The only difference in this case is that the pip remains stationary and the squeezer (the chameleon's tongue) is shot out.

But what happens at the front end of the tongue?

The tip is club shaped and slathered in thick, sticky saliva – the consistency almost like that of honey. Furthermore, a loose flap of skin that trails behind the tip of the tongue packs an additional punch when it shoots forward on impact and partially envelopes the prey to trap it against the sticky tip.

With the prey trapped on the tip, the long, extended tongue now simply flops down. Another set of muscles on the back of the tongue, called retractor muscles, 'reel' the tongue back in and over the tapered bone. The retrieval process is much slower than the forward-shooting motion.

Tongue now again firmly in cheek, the firing assembly is reset and the chameleon starts chewing its prey.

But there's more involved in catching an unsuspecting insect than simply shooting out a sticky tongue. Owing to the immense forces involved in supporting the tongue's mechanism, special tendons are necessary to protect the muscles from shock, tears or snapping off completely.

Extreme accuracy is also crucial to lock onto the target. With both eyes focused on the prey, the chameleon does some clever calculations, computing the height at which it needs to aim for the length of its tongue to reach the prey and aiming its head perfectly to compensate for the curve (due to gravity) along which the tongue must travel through the air.

Sometimes, when it works out that the prey will be just out of range, the chameleon will inch forward almost imperceptibly. With its back legs and tail anchored firmly onto the tip of a branch, it will lean gracefully out into space to make up the required shortfall in range . . . and then take the shot.

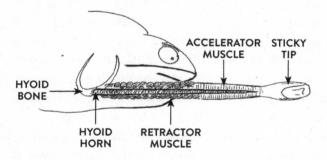

The components of a chameleon's tongue.

If a chameleon's eyes work independently of each other, how does it make sense of what it sees?

A chameleon's eyes are most intriguing. Resembling mini concrete mixers on either side of the head, they swivel around completely independently of one another. This means that one eye sees a completely different picture from the other (the eyes are said to be 'uncoupled').

Although it seems like a dizzying mechanism, the chameleon is able to cover 360 degrees while keeping an eye out for prey or possible danger. The eye movements also mean the animal can keep on edging forward very slowly without turning its head, allowing it to move along almost imperceptibly.

Chameleon eyes move indepedently. Each eye knows what the other eye is watching.

When one of the eyes does spot a potential catch, it immediately locks onto the prey. At the same time, the brain alerts the other eye to synchronise with the one on target – a process called 'coupling'. It's almost like being able to watch two different movies in your head at the same time, but being able to shut one down and watch the other for a while if you need to.

Only once both eyes are trained on the target does the head rotate slowly to allow a full visual lock, shifting from monocular to binocular vision. This is critical for getting the tongue to shoot out accurately, as explained earlier.

CROCODILES

Must they swallow rocks to grind up their food and control their buoyancy?

No, this is a myth, even though rocks have been found in the stomachs of some crocodiles, which may have led people to believe they *need* to swallow rocks to survive.

Old crocodile hunters will tell you that stones are rarely found in the guts of crocodiles. In fact, in areas such as the Okavango Swamps, stones are few and far between. Some crocodiles may never see a rock in their entire lifetime. So how significant, if at all, is this stone intake for their survival?

I've often been told by guides on safari that crocodiles swallow stones or rocks, and I have no doubt that they have been seen swallowing rocks. But the jury is still out whether this is done expressly in order to control buoyancy and to grind their food.

Many animals are known to ingest stones. These stomach or gizzard stones are called gastroliths (from the Greek *gastro*, meaning 'stomach', and *lithos*, meaning 'stone'). They're normally ingested by animals that don't have grinding teeth, like crocodiles (birds are another good example), and serve to grind food in the gizzard, aiding its digestibility. Dinosaur fossils containing gastroliths have in fact been found.

However, opinions differ when it comes to rocks in crocs. Those in support of the 'rocks-for-ballast' theory say that the added weight of the swallowed stones:

- makes the croc heavier, enabling it to overpower and drown prey more easily
- makes the animal less susceptible to currents
- submerges its body underwater, leaving only the eyes and snout exposed
- enables a crocodile to dive deeper and to stay underwater for longer, because with a heavier body it can take in more air and still sink.

But none of these ideas have been unequivocally proven. In fact, research has proven some of them outright improbable. For example, studies by the palaeontologist Don Henderson show that a buoyancy stabilisation effect would kick in only if a crocodile had swallowed at least 6% of its own body mass in rocks. The heaviest recorded Nile crocodile (which weighed over 1 000 kg) would therefore have needed to ingest 60 kg of rock.

In addition, one would have to consider how a crocodile would know where to find suitable rocks and how much they would need to ingest to get their buoyancy just right.

It seems unlikely then that rocks are swallowed for the sole purpose of buoyancy control or as gastroliths. Perhaps they're merely swallowed incidentally while the croc is picking up scraps, as they often do?

Do crocodiles store their prey to rot in lairs before feeding?

It's commonly believed that after crocodiles have killed their prey, they will transfer the carcass into a secret underground lair, often in or under a river bank, or hide the prey in a safe place where it can decay to a such an extent that it is easy to tear apart.

But this is a misconception, which probably comes from crocodiles not having cutting teeth and so not being able to tear chunks of flesh from a dead animal, nor being able to chew because their jaws cannot move from side to side, only up and down.

To remove flesh from a carcass, a crocodile needs to lock on to a chunk of flesh and forcefully rip it free or spin its entire body to do so. Perhaps putrid flesh that would just fall off the bone would be a much easier option, hence the idea that crocodiles would consciously store their prey so that decomposition can take place.

However, the truth is that although crocodiles have been observed eating putrid flesh, it's not their first preference. In fact, those in the know will tell you that baiting crocodile traps with fresh rather than rotting meat yields most success.

Is the sex of a crocodile determined genetically?

In most animals, sex is determined by sex chromosomes at the time of fertilisation. But this is not so for crocodiles – their lot as a male or a female is determined by the temperature of the environment in which they were incubated as eggs.

Eggs of the Nile crocodile take around three months to hatch. Females of this species are extremely protective of their nests and their young. Should a nesting site prove to be safe and successful, a female may use that same site for the rest of her life, if undisturbed.

Eggs incubated at a temperature of 26–30 °C during a certain window of development will lead to females developing, while temperatures higher than 31 °C will lead to males hatching from the eggs. In a narrow band somewhere between the low and high temperatures, it's possible that both males and females can hatch from the same clutch of eggs.

All crocodilians and most tortoises and sea turtles appear to be subject to this phenomenon of temperature-dependent gender determination.

Do crocodiles shed tears?

The expression 'crying crocodile tears', which means that someone insincerely shows grief or sadness, may go back hundreds of years. Some writings from the 13th and 14th centuries suggest that crocodiles treacherously shed tears to lure sympathetic victims closer before snatching them, or that they cried tears of delight while feasting.

The fact is that crocodiles do have tears – all vertebrates do in some form – and they have been recorded shedding tears. Tears prevent the eyes from drying out and thus are essential for ensuring good eyesight. The composition of tears doesn't differ that much across species, with all tears comprising three main ingredients: a saline solution of minerals and proteins, mucus and oil. This fluid not only lubricates and nourishes the eyes, but also helps to prevent infection and dryness, and flushes out impurities.

But back to the reason for crocodile tears. Research shows that some crocodiles, such as alligators and caimans in the Americas, do shed tears while feeding, but I don't know if this is true for all crocodilians of the world. (Caimans are any of several species of Central and South American crocodilian related to alligators.) The studies were done on a small sample of captive alligators and caimans in a reptile park. They were fed in a dry area well away from water and filmed closely. Footage showed that most of the animals actually did shed tears while feeding, and some even had frothy 'bubbles' of tears spilling out of their eyes.

The reason for this is not clear, but scientists suggest that it could be related to the huffing, puffing and hissing of these particular crocodilians while they're feeding. It's possible, they say, that all this blowing could affect the sinuses, causing overproduction of tears.

Humans are the only creatures known to readily shed tears in response to emotion. Apart from basal tears (those that bathe our eyes all day) and reflex tears (produced to flush away irritants, like when chopping an onion), we can be moved to tears by a sad movie, fear, anger, joy and a host of other emotions. That's why humans can produce 50–130 litres of tears in a lifetime.

Final answer? Yes, some crocodiles can shed tears, but it's not because they're sad about tearing apart their prey.

🐸 FROGS AND TOADS

Do you get warts if you touch them?

No, it's an old wives' tale. Common warts in humans are the result of a skin infection caused by certain types of human papillomavirus. The virus causes a rapid, localised growth of cells, which we call a wart. The infection is extremely contagious, and warts can readily spread between people and to other parts of the body.

Because some frogs and toads have warty bumps on their skin, many people believe they're the same as the warts we see in humans, and that they must be contagious. They're not.

But that's not to say that the bumps on a toad's body are not without some danger, specifically the parotoid glands (poison glands on the neck or shoulder of some toads). Toads are sitting ducks for predators, especially when they're on dry land. As they're not particularly speedy animals, they need an alternative mechanism of defence. These parotoid glands can secrete substances called bufotoxins, which are their major weapon to deter predators. I've seen a few dogs that sincerely regretted attempting to bite a toad (if their facial contortions are anything to go by).

Technically, almost all frogs and toads are poisonous to some degree because of toxins produced by glands in their skin. In South Africa, two types of toad produce skin secretions that are potentially fatal to animals and humans. In South America, some of the tiny poison dart frogs produce a toxin so potent that only a fraction of a gram can potentially kill a human. The poison has been used for centuries on the tips of forest hunters' blowgun darts.

So, while frogs and toads do not cause warts, it's nonetheless best practice not to touch them.

GECKOS

How do geckos stick to vertical surfaces?

Not by sticky secretions, suction cups or tiny hooks. They adhere to surfaces because of minute hairs on their toes, specialised foot tendons and weak electrostatic forces (called Van der Waals forces).

Although not all geckos are able to stick to walls, the real stick(l)ers have thousands of microscopic hairs (called setae) on each foot. Each hair, in turn, may have around 1 000 frayed ends, which gives a gecko millions of setae end points.

This is where the Van der Waals forces come in. In a nutshell, a Van der Waals force is a weak electrostatic force that holds molecules together. It is generated when fluctuating charge distribution between adjacent molecules sync.

With the millions of setae end points, these weak intermolecular forces combine to the extent that a gecko can stick to a surface with a force equivalent to 10 atmospheres of pressure!

This poses another problem, though: how does a gecko then pry its 'stuck' foot *off* the wall? Geckos know the solution is simple: instead of yanking the foot off, they know they have to *peel* it off by turning the toes at a certain angle, much as you'd peel a strip of adhesive tape off a surface.

Pulling a piece of tape off a surface usually requires a slow and steady action, but geckos can attach and detach their feet at an astonishing rate of 15 times per second when they run. They manage this because foot tendons attached directly to the skin ensure that the feet are perfectly stiffened during even the briefest surface contact, so that there's always a maximum distribution of adhesive forces.

When geckos are shedding their skin or if stuff is stuck in their setae, the Van der Waals forces don't work that well and they struggle to stick to a surface. They're also unable to adhere to a surface that's covered in dust, moisture or oil, or has a non-stick coating like Teflon.

SNAKES: GENERAL

Why are people so scared of snakes?

People have an irrational fear of snakes. Blind terror, hysteria and panic-stricken efforts to escape are commonplace if a snake is spotted. The mere thought or mention of a snake can bring on an intense physiological anxiety in some people, a condition known as ophidiophobia (from the Greek *ophis*, meaning 'snake or serpent', and *phobos*, meaning 'fear'). It's so acute in some people that they require medication and treatment for their fear.

But where does people's fear and loathing of snakes come from?

- **Learned behaviour:** People are often taught – indeed encouraged – to fear snakes (think of how people say 'the only good snake is a dead snake!') and often they're associated with harm, death and evil. (The Bible mentions snakes close to 200 times.) Since children are particularly receptive to such negative descriptions, parents and teachers should try to allay these fears.
- **Pop culture:** Oh, the number of scary snake movies! Think of *Anaconda*, *Snakes on a Plane*, *Python*, *Piranhaconda*, *Sssssss* . . . Even the brave Indiana Jones was afraid only of snakes; Harry Potter bravely slayed the Serpent of Slytherin and a wide-eyed Mowgli wrapped in the terrifying coils of Kaa in *The Jungle Book* made us all sit on the edge of our seats. None of these images help to convince people that snakes are not scary.
- **Your own or someone else's bad experience with a snake:** People love to regale others with scary tales of how they, or someone they know, narrowly 'escaped certain death' after a confrontation with a snake.

So, let's set the record straight by distinguishing between fact and fallacy when it comes to snakes:

- According to Johan Marais of the African Snakebite Institute, there are 173 snake species in southern Africa, of which only 19 (11%) are considered deadly to humans. Although 173 species might seem a lot, it's less than half the number you would find in Brazil (375) and about a hundred fewer than in India (275). Ireland, New Zealand, Iceland, Alaska and Siberia are naturally snake free (as are the sunnier small islands in the Pacific).

- More people are struck by lightning annually than are bitten by venomous snakes.
- Snakes are not slimy or wet; they're dry and mostly smooth to the touch.
- Snakes aren't 'out to get you'. They tend to flee rather than fight and would not intentionally chase after a person. If a snake did appear to 'chase' someone, it was undoubtedly because both equally startled snake and human coincidentally chose the same escape route at the time.
- Snakes do not travel in pairs. So, when a snake is killed, its 'partner' will not hunt you down (it's a Bollywood myth). Nor will a dying snake 'keep a picture of you in its eye' so that its mate can find you to wreak revenge.
- Snakes that have been beheaded will not die only after the sun has gone down.
- Snakes do not need to be burned to ensure that they're dead. (This misconception is presumably due to the rinkhals's habit of feigning death when severely threatened or injured – more about that later.)
- Pythons do not lie in wait in trees to drop onto and kill unsuspecting prey passing below.
- Snakes do not lick their prey to cover it in saliva for lubrication to aid swallowing.
- A snake's tongue cannot sting you.
- Snakes cannot hypnotise their prey. This idea probably stems from observations that small animals 'freeze' in fear at the approach of a snake.
- Snakes do not use their tails as whips to lash out in defence.
- Snake repellents will *not* keep snakes away. Neither will petrol, Jeyes fluid, mothballs or even dogs.
- Not all snakes found in trees are boomslangs, nor are all green

PART 3: REPTILES AND AMPHIBIANS

snakes in trees green mambas. In South Africa, green mambas are found only in a narrow strip of coastline forest from the most northern parts of the Eastern Cape into KwaZulu-Natal.

- Snakes don't form hoops by biting their tails in order to roll away from or after you.
- Snakes do not milk cows, nor are they attracted to saucers of milk (which have supposedly been used as bait to trap them).
- Removing a snake's fangs does not render it harmless. Lost or broken fangs are constantly replaced in some species. Others (like puff adders) even have 'reserve' fangs that swing into position to replace fangs that may have been broken off inside their prey.

What is the most dangerous snake in South Africa?

The answer is not that simple: there's a difference between the most *dangerous* and the most *venomous* when it comes to snakes.

Take, for example, the boomslang (*Dispholidus typus*). A boomslang has the most potent venom of any snake in Africa. Its venom yield (the amount of venom delivered by a snake when it bites) is around 8 mg, of which about a hundredth (0.07 mg) is enough to kill a human. By comparison, a black mamba's venom yield is almost 40 times greater (300 mg) and an amount about 200 times greater (15 mg) is needed to kill a human.

But despite its extremely potent venom, a boomslang has a most docile demeanour; it rarely bites. I've witnessed a boomslang in a bush being tirelessly molested by a bunch of oafish plonkers, who were poking, jabbing and teasing it with a floppy hat tied to a long stick. All that the snake did was to inflate its neck in the hope that the threat would go away, and try its utmost to hide or flee from this unnecessary and unwanted intrusion. No amount of harassment was able to provoke the snake into any form of retaliation, not even once. I managed to dissuade the 'attackers' from their onslaught and we watched the boomslang beat a hasty retreat.

In contrast, the demeanour of a black mamba is quite different: it's extremely cautious, if not jittery. Like any snake, it prefers flight over fight, but if threatened or cornered, it won't hesitate to retaliate with bold intent. Black mambas bite readily, often repeatedly, and just by virtue of their size (the longest one recorded was over 4 m) are able to deliver large amounts of mostly neurotoxic, quick-acting venom – severe effects are experienced in minutes rather than hours. However, the common belief that people *die* within minutes from a mamba bite is untrue. According to Johan Marias it would take 4–16 hours for a human to die after being bitten by a black mamba.

So, whereas a boomslang may be the most venomous, the black mamba (or 'maarhmber', as they pronounce it in KwaZulu-Natal) is arguably the most *dangerous* snake in southern Africa.

Boomslang (left) and black mamba (right).

Can snakes think?

Many people have the unfortunate idea that snakes are primitive, brainless venom machines programmed only to bite and kill, and are incapable of any cognitive function other than that. This may even stem partly from the scientific literature that emerged in the 1950s about the so-called 'reptilian' (or 'lizard') brain, capable only of the four Fs: flight, flee, feed and fornicate.

However, there's now overwhelming evidence that snakes (and reptiles in general) have a much greater cerebral ability than was previously thought, particularly when it comes to learning.

In this regard, I'm completely fascinated by the remarkable anti-predator strategy known as thanatosis – shamming death – and intrigued by the deeper implications that can be inferred about animal behaviour with regard to their 'understanding' the concept of death.

Does the rinkhals actually *know* and understand that it is feigning death, or is this just a life-preserving evolutionary adaptation, hard-wired to kick in automatically when the chips are down? Whatever the reason, this behaviour may be a strong manifestation of how widely understood the concept of death is in nature.

Humans arrogantly like to believe that we are the only creatures capable of fully grasping the concept of mortality. In fact, we claim our very awareness of death and mortality as one of the characteristics that sets us apart from the rest of the animal kingdom. Well, thanatosis, for one, blows a hole in this conceit.

Looking at the death-feigning rinkhals, perhaps we should re-consider the philosophies we use to justify our human sense of self-importance. The concept of death appears to be grasped not only by the rinkhals, but also by its attackers or predators. And clearly, it works – that's why it evolved.

In her book *Schrödinger's Opossum*, Susana Monsó, a researcher at the Spanish National University of Distance Education, writes that although we like to think of ourselves as a unique species, the traits on which we base this concept of uniqueness are starting to fall as science reveals the staggering diversity and complexity of animal minds and behaviour. There's now solid evidence of culture, morality, rationality and even rudimentary forms of 'language' in the animal kingdom.

In her view, we can no longer resort to the concept of death to convince ourselves of how very special we are. It is time to rethink the idea of human exceptionalism and the disrespect for the natural world that comes with it.

Are snakes deaf?

No. Just because they don't have external ears and don't seem to react to sound does not mean that they can't hear.

Humans are able to hear because sound waves hitting the eardrum are transmitted to the inner ear, where tiny hairs connected to nerve cells vibrate and so initiate nerve impulses that are sent to the brain.

Snakes may not have external ears or an eardrum, but they do have a well-developed inner ear. Instead of their inner ear being connected to an eardrum (like ours), it's connected to their jawbone. Since the jawbone is in contact with the ground, it can detect even the most minute vibrations passing through the ground. These vibrations, such as the footsteps of a predator or prey, are translated into signals that are sent to the brain via the inner ear. So, a snake 'hears' by taking it on the chin! There's also evidence that snakes have specialised sense organs in the skin and along the length of the body that are able to detect vibrations.

So acute is this method of 'hearing' in some snakes that they can accurately pinpoint and attack a mouse purely by picking up on the vibrations caused by it. Desert horned vipers (*Cerastes cerastes*) are apparently masters at this. It's been proposed that snakes that bury themselves in the sand (like the desert horned viper) may do so not only to hide or protect themselves, but also to better detect vibrations since they have overall body contact with the soil in which they're buried – like a living seismometer.

So, snakes are able to detect vibrations on the ground, but can they also pick up sound waves travelling through the air? It seems so, yes, although they're not very good at it. Within a limited range of frequencies, airborne sound waves cause the skull of the snake to vibrate. These vibrations are then translated by the inner ear into signals that are sent to the brain.

Some years ago, I was fortunate enough to experience a snake's astonishing sensitivity to vibrations first hand. While inspecting orchards on my farm just outside White River, I blundered into a snouted cobra (*Naja annulifera*, previously known as the Egyptian cobra). It was a magnificent specimen, close to 2 m long and in perfect condition. The wary snake, less than 3 m away, immediately reared up to face me with an impressive hood raised high off the ground. I froze on the spot and we eye-balled each other, keeping dead still, for what seemed like several minutes.

When the cobra realised that I posed no threat, it lowered itself from its hooded stance and slowly moved off. So thrilled was I by this experience that I immediately called a colleague working in the farm office not 300 m away, telling her to come quickly and share this rare sighting. 'On my way!' she said, and bolted from the office in our direction.

Snouted cobra.

I was following the snake, walking slowly a few metres behind it. It was completely relaxed and seemed totally unconcerned by my presence. Then suddenly, as my running colleague approached to within about 30 m of us, the snake immediately reared up again, turning to face the direction of the approaching person, who, amazingly, was still hidden from view behind the trees in the orchard. Neither I nor the snake could see her running towards us at the moment the snake reared up to face her approach.

It remained so for only a few seconds before violently beating a thrashing retreat, passing only a metre from where I was standing.

The amazing ability of snakes to sense our approach is part of the reason that we so seldom see them in the bush. Oh, they're there, all right . . . But most (bar puff adders and a few others) move away on sensing us long before we're close enough to see them.

Can snakes dislocate their jaws?

The ability of snakes to swallow what seems like impossibly large prey is the stuff of morbid fascination and no doubt contributes to the nightmarish horror associated with 'serpents'. But it is incorrectly believed that snakes can dislocate, detach, unhinge or disengage their jaws from their skull.

In the absence of cutting teeth and limbs with which they can chop prey into manageable portions, snakes need to swallow their prey whole, even if it's several times bigger than the snake's head. That's why they have developed a few remarkable adaptations that render their jaws 'expandable'. Their jawbones are agile and operate independently of each other, which allows them to be manoeuvred around oversized prey. In addition, their elastic skin can stretch over oversized prey as it is manipulated into their body.

Snakes' ability to open their mouths wide is due to the jawbones not being tightly joined together like in mammals, but instead being connected by a stretchy ligament. The front ends of the mandibles (lower jaws) spread wide apart, away from each other. A good way to visualise this is to think of moving your index and middle fingers apart to form a V-shape, with your nails being the front of the jawbones where the ligament is attached. The back ends of the jawbones therefore also need loose, elastic connections to the skull to allow for the extended lateral movement of the front ends.

QUADRATE BONE
Attaching the back of the lower jaw to the skull, the quadrate bone can hinge vertically and horizontally to accommodate large prey.

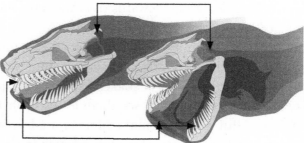

CURVED TEETH
The teeth are curved backwards towards the throat. They hook and hold the prey, preventing it from escaping.

ELASTIC LIGAMENT
The ligament joining the lower mandibles stretches, allowing each mandible to move independently to 'walk' food into its throat.

How snakes swallow large prey.

To swallow prey, the snake 'walks' its head over the prey by alternately edging the jaws on each side of the head forward, over the body of the prey. The numerous backward-pointing teeth grip the prey on one side, while the other side inches forward to grip and anchor. Then the other side moves forward, gripping and anchoring. This one-side-then-the-other-side action is repeated over and over until the head of the snake has fully engulfed the prey. It's usually a slow and laborious process, especially when the prey is large.

Once the prey has been manoeuvred to reach the gullet behind the head, muscle contractions in this region of the body take over, pushing the prey down into the stomach for digestion.

Have humans been swallowed by snakes? Yes, mostly by reticulated pythons (*Malayopython reticulatus*), a species that occurs in Indonesia. In 2017, a 25-year-old man was killed and eaten by a reticulated python. In the following year the same thing happened to a 54-year-old woman. Reticulated pythons are the longest snakes in the world, and an individual of 9.6 metres has apparently been recorded.

Do all snakes eat eggs?

When it comes to eggs being part of a snake's diet, the impression may exist that either only one type of snake eats eggs (hence the name 'egg eater') or that all snakes eat eggs. Which is true?

To understand the answer, consider first that we can divide snakes into two groups: those that *specialise* in eating eggs and those that don't. Among those that are not specially adapted to eat eggs are some that will eat an egg if the opportunity arises (because they can) and those that don't eat any eggs . . . ever (because they simply can't).

The specialist egg eaters are then divided further into those that eat bird eggs and those that prefer reptile eggs.

So, in summary, there are four categories: snakes that do not, ever, eat eggs; those that do eat eggs, but only sometimes; those that primarily eat bird eggs and those that primarily eat reptile eggs.

◎ **Snakes that eat bird eggs:** There are three species of these specialist egg eaters in South Africa, of which the most common and widespread is the common (or rhombic) egg eater (*Dasypeltis scabra*). Seldom longer than a metre in length, they can swallow bird eggs with a diameter about three times greater than their own heads. They're able to accomplish this feat because of the extremely

141

elastic skin of the lower jaw and neck, which enables the head to stretch over and easily envelope the entire egg. The swallowed egg is then pushed towards the gullet by muscle contractions.

A neat trick then happens. The vertebrae in the neck have specially modified bony spines that protrude downwards – dagger-like – into the gullet. As the egg is forced back against the bones, the spines grind into the shell, effectively 'sawing' into it lengthways. This cutting action, together with the squeezing and gyrating muscle contractions, crushes the egg, causing it to collapse under pressure in the snake's throat. The liquid contents of the egg are released and swallowed. The neatly flattened eggshell casing, still intact and held together by the egg membrane, is regurgitated, as a complete but flattened package (like a beach ball that's been deflated and flattened).

Common egg eater eating a bird egg (left) and reguritating an eggshell (right).

Being virtually toothless, venomless and not really built for speedy getaways, the common egg eater is rather vulnerable and defenceless. But it compensates for these inadequacies by closely mimicking the coloration of the common or rhombic night adder (*Causus rhombeatus*), with which it is often confused and is therefore summarily killed. The reverse is also true: some people mistake a venomous night adder for a harmless egg eater, pick it up and get bitten.

As part of its ruse, the common egg eater will put up a ferocious defence display when threatened. With a continuous looping or winding action against itself, coiling and uncoiling, its rough, serrated scales rub against each other to produce a loud hissing sound, just like the warning hiss of some venomous adders. At the same time, it repeatedly lashes out with vicious (but toothless – shame!) strikes, mouth agape to expose a black lining, like that of a black mamba.

It's an impressive and convincing routine to behold as this completely harmless, mild-mannered little creature pulls off the performance of its life to save that same life.

Common egg eater (left) and common night adder (right).

◉ **Snakes that eat reptile eggs:** These are the shovel-snout snakes (genus *Prosymna*), of which there are seven species in southern Africa. They're small (about 30 cm long) and burrow in loose soil, hence the shovel-like structure on their snouts. They feed almost exclusively on the eggs of small snakes and lizards, which are swallowed whole. Shovel-snouts lack fangs and venom, and are completely harmless to humans.

Sundevall's shovel-snout, showing the shovel used to burrow in sand. They feed almost exclusively on reptile eggs.

143

⦿ **Opportunistic egg eaters:** These are snakes that do not specialise in eating eggs, whether from birds or reptiles, but will do so when they have a chance. They have no specialised mechanism to crush bird eggs and ingest their contents like the true egg eaters do. Eggs are simply swallowed and digested, shell and all. Many a hen house has been raided by egg-eating cobras. Boomslangs will also eat bird eggs if found, and a population of mole snakes on Robben Island feed almost exclusively on the eggs of ground-nesting birds such as gulls and penguins.

Do snakes in southern Africa hibernate in winter?

The term 'hibernation' is a term that refers to the regular state of dormancy that some vertebrates adopt in order to survive severe winter conditions. They do this by lowering their body temperature and metabolic activities, becoming inactive and sleeping throughout the bitterly cold months. True hibernators can reach states where they appear to be dead, with their heartbeats barely perceptible, only a few shallow breaths heard per minute and their body temperature dropping to close to 0 °C. (That's why bears are not considered true hibernators: although they sleep through the cold months, their body temperature barely drops.)

It's a misconception that reptiles – including snakes – do this. It simply doesn't get cold enough in southern Africa for them to go into true hibernation. Instead they go into a state of torpor (inactivity) in times of cold weather. In extremely cold regions of the world, hundreds or even thousands of snakes will share the same protective shelter as they weather adverse conditions for months on end.

Snakes are cold-blooded animals (also called ectotherms), which means that they rely entirely on external sources in the environment, such as sunlight or warm rock surfaces, to control their body temperature. When temperatures drop in southern Africa during the winter months, snakes will seek shelter from the cold in any warm location, such as termite mounds or animal burrows, where warmth is retained several metres underground. They become sluggish or fairly inactive at low temperatures, but will re-emerge on warm days to bask in the sun, often near or just outside their temporary refuge. When the temperature becomes uncomfortably cold again, they'll return to their warmer lairs to wait out the cold spell.

Since there is comparatively little food available to snakes during winter, they build up fat reserves to tide them over during the less active winter months. In fact, they can easily endure an entire winter without feeding at all (some snakes can survive for well over a year without food). Being ectotherms, they don't require as much food as warm-blooded animals (endotherms), which need to feed regularly to maintain a constant body temperature. Egg-eating snakes, in particular, are a good example of this behaviour, as birds' eggs are readily available to them only during the warmer spring or summer months.

So, contrary to belief, winter in South Africa is not a time when 'all the snakes have disappeared because they're hibernating', as I've often been told. Snakes are always around, appreciating the warm, sunny days in winter just as any self-respecting South African would do.

Do some snakes pretend to be dead when threatened?

Yes, and the rinkhals (*Hemachatus haemachatus*) is probably the most well-known trickster. But it's not the only snake that feigns death – other species in South Africa, such as the striped skaapsteker (*Psammophylax tritaeniatus*), the Natal black snake (*Macrelaps microlepidotus*) and the snouted cobra (*Naja annulifera*), also resort to this deceptive behaviour.

When a rinkhals is threatened, its first line of defence is normally to beat a hasty retreat from the threat. When cornered, its second line of defence kicks in and it will literally take a stand, raising almost half of its body off the ground while spreading a wide, impressive hood. (This is typically when the cream or white bands on the contrasting black underside of the raised neck are seen, hence the name 'rinkhals', meaning 'ring neck' in Afrikaans.) It's from this raised position that a rinkhals may attempt to spit, lunging forward and hissing loudly as it does so.

As a last resort, the rinkhals may pretend to be dead. And this performance is remarkably convincing. It rolls over, often with the entire body upside down, mouth agape, tongue hanging out . . . and lies still, dead still. If picked up while shamming death, it may remain limp – or it may suddenly 'come to life' and bite. Beware!

Playing dead (thanatosis, from the Greek *thanatos*, which means 'death') is not uncommon in the animal kingdom. It's not the same as tonic immobility, though, which is a kind of paralysis – a rigid, unmoving state in response to the perception of inescapable danger causing prey to 'freeze', often at the approach of a predator.

Death feigning is normally done only as an absolute last resort. There are several theories as to why the behaviour exists. Perhaps playing dead is intended to stop the onslaught by the attacker (who has been made to believe that the prey does not need to be subdued any further or that it's successfully neutralised a threat). Not only would this prevent further damage to the 'dead' victim, but the respite may also provide the 'corpse' with an opportunity to escape.

Although the questions about *why* thanatosis is performed or *how* it evolved remain unanswered, there is little doubt that this extraordinary illusory ploy works – and very well.

Rinkhals feigning death.

146

SNAKES AND THEIR BITES

Which snakes are responsible for the most bites in southern Africa?

It's often believed that if you're bitten by a venomous snake, it's tickets. But this is rarely the case. In fact, some statistics peg you as being nine times more likely to die from a lightning strike than a snake strike.

From the outset, it's important to make the distinction between *snakebites* and *deaths* due to snakebites. Of the estimated 10–12 fatalities in southern Africa each year, most are caused by bites from the Cape cobra (*Naja nivea*) and the black mamba (*Dendroaspis polylepis*). Their predominantly neurotoxic venom has a rapid effect on breathing.

If we're talking only about bites, not deaths, then the most common snakebites in southern Africa are caused by Mozambique spitting cobras (*mfezi* in isiZulu), puff adders, night adders and stiletto snakes (but not necessarily in this order).

- **Mozambique spitting cobra:** Juveniles especially seem to have a distinct propensity for visiting homesteads, and because of the high probability of coming into contact with humans, their pets or livestock, bites or incidents of eye envenomation are frequently reported (these cobras react readily if they feel threatened).

  Fatalities from bites of Mozambique spitting cobras are extremely rare – only a few deaths have been recorded – but the potent cytotoxic venom can cause severe tissue damage that can necessitate skin grafts and amputations.

  Some people contend that while on the hunt for food, snakes will only attack or bite prey that falls within their prey size: in other words, prey of a size that they are able to swallow. This does not seem to hold true for Mozambique spitting cobras, as they've been proven to bite objects impossibly beyond their prey size.

  Take sleeping humans as an example. There are many recorded instances where these unfortunate victims have been bitten despite posing no threat to the snake nor accidentally rolling onto it in their sleep, causing it to bite in defence or retaliation. (I know of one case where a man, fast asleep, had his arm dangling harmlessly and almost motionlessly off the bed when this snake bit him, delivering a solid bite with full envenomation.) The snakes are unlikely to have been in search of heat, as these bites occurred on hot nights. There are also stories of children that are reputed to have been bitten in the face while asleep, their flickering eyelids blamed for triggering the attack. Who knows whether this is true.

It seems that when it comes to food, Mozambique spitting cobras may suffer from low impulse control, and may have a go at anything – even if it's motionless, unthreatening or way too big to swallow.

Mozambique spitting cobra.

- **Puff adder:** Puff adders are often made out to be the culprits causing the most deaths by snakebite in South Africa. But the truth is that fatalities from puff adder bites are rare. Since these snakes are one of the most widespread and common species in our region, it's not surprising that many bites from puff adders are recorded – especially among sugar cane workers – but only a tiny proportion of the bites are fatal. The fatalities that do occur are usually because the bites were not treated properly, leading to sepsis (puff adders have cytotoxic venom).

Puff adder.

◉ **Night adders:** Two types of night adder occur in South Africa, namely the common (or rhombic) night adder (*Causus rhombeatus*) and the snouted night adder (*Causus defilippii*). They're common within their ranges and, like the Mozambique spitting cobra, are well known for frequenting and entering homesteads in search of warmth, food or shelter. Generally, they have a docile nature, much preferring to flee rather than fight, but in the face of a threat they'll strike out with an impressive and vicious display.

Because of their association with human habitation, and perhaps also because they're easily confused with the harmless common (or rhombic) egg eater (see an earlier entry), which could lead to people picking them up, bites from this species are not uncommon.

The easiest way to differentiate between a rhombic night adder and its harmless egg-eating lookalike is that the night adder has a bold and distinct V-shaped marking on the top of its head, while the egg eater's head is mottled on top.

There are no reports of anyone having died from a night adder bite. There are, however, reported cases of dogs supposedly having been killed by night adders. Their venom causes pain and swelling, and will require medical attention.

◉ **Stiletto snakes:** Most bites inflicted by these snakes (from the genus *Atractaspis*, and also called burrowing asps, side-stabbing snakes or mole vipers) occur while they are being handled. They're notorious for this, and the reason is twofold.

Firstly, stiletto snakes are often mistaken by amateur snake catchers for one of the harmless varieties of thread or blind snakes, or even legless skinks. They've even been mistaken for brown house snakes (though they bear no resemblance). If a stiletto snake is handled unguardedly in a case of mistaken identity, a bite is bound to happen – it's almost a given.

Secondly, stiletto snakes bite in a most unconventional and unexpected way. Their 'bite' is actually better described as a peculiar, lateral stabbing action. Their long fangs are brought into play sideways (not downwards, as is the norm) from the front of the upper jaw. The snake effectively 'hooks' a fang into the attacker or prey by flexing its very supple head sideways. It needn't even open its mouth fully when jabbing a fang horizontally. This makes stiletto snakes extremely tricky, if not almost impossible, to hold safely behind the head without a very good chance of taking a hit, which is why even expert snake handlers get bitten, accounting for a large proportion of recorded bites.

Bibron's stiletto snake.

Even though their venom contains a potent cytotoxin, no one has ever died from a stiletto snake's bite. Be prepared, however, for excruciating pain, blistering, swelling and the possible loss of a finger or two, together with lifelong tissue scarring, if you're bitten. The best advice is never to handle any snake unless you're absolutely sure what it is, the reason for handling it is totally unavoidable or you're completely confident and experienced in handling snakes.

What's the difference between poisonous, venomous and toxic snakes?

The first question a snake handler is usually asked is, 'Is it poisonous?!' Snakes are not poisonous – they're venomous. Yet the terms 'poisonous', 'venomous' and 'toxic' are often mistakenly used as synonyms. Add 'toxin' and 'toxicants' into the mix and there's even more confusion.

Here's the low-down:

- Toxins are biologically produced chemical substances that can adversely affect you.
- Toxicants are human-made chemical substances that can adversely affect you.
- Something is poisonous if it secretes a toxin that can poison you when you eat, inhale or touch it. Basically, if *you bite it* and you die (or are hurt, at the very least), it's poisonous. Examples are poisonous plants (such as the arum lily or the delicious monster) or the skin of some frogs (like the toads discussed earlier).
- Something is venomous if it injects (via fangs, spines, a sting and so on) a toxin into its prey's body, such as a snake (bite) or a scorpion (sting). Basically, if *it bites you* and you die (or are hurt badly), it's venomous.

Can snakes deliver a 'dry' bite?

This is indeed possible. But contrary to belief, they don't 'dry bite' because they were in a good mood or feeling 'kind' at the time!

Many tales are told in wide-eyed wonder of people who are purportedly 'fortunate to be alive' after their encounter with a venomous snake because the benevolent serpent 'decided' on the day not to kill them, and delivered a dry bite instead.

'Dry bite' is a term used to describe a bite from any creature (including spiders or scorpions) in which no venom is delivered into the tissues of the victim. By way of explanation, a bite from a non-venomous snake is considered to be dry, as no venom is delivered. (This doesn't mean that bites from non-venomous snakes are completely harmless – their teeth can break off inside your skin or harmful bacteria in their mouths can cause secondary infections.)

But it's the venomous snakes that are normally the subject of the wild speculation that follows dry bites. People seem to be fascinated by the idea that snakes are endowed with the ability to 'choose' whether or not to kill, by injecting or withholding venom at will during a bite. And this quandary has for many resulted in their profuse and lifelong thanks to providence for still being alive after being bitten by a deadly snake, curiously with no symptoms or signs of envenomation. Their ordeal and luck, they say, can be attributed to the dry bite phenomenon. (Bear in mind that in many, if not most cases, they might well have been bitten by a harmless snake that was incorrectly identified as being a venomous species.)

There are a number of reasons why a venomous snake may have delivered a dry bite: its venom glands may be empty or inactive due to infection or damage; venom ducts from the venom glands could be blocked; the hollow, needle-like fangs could be blocked, often due to calcification of the venom canal or the fangs could be absent, having been broken off due to trauma. It's not uncommon for aged snakes to suffer from these afflictions.

It's also possible that owing to insufficient reach or the angle of the strike, the snake wasn't able to embed its fangs into flesh, despite the victim both seeing and feeling the 'hit'. Clothing can also be responsible for obstructing bites or incomplete fang penetration. In fact, research has shown that denim clothing can reduce envenomation by 66% in rattlesnake bites. There's no doubt that wearing suitable shoes or boots and long trousers instead of shorts can go a long way to reducing the severity of snakebites.

Some snakes may even lash out boldly as a warning or deterrent with their mouths closed. Or if striking purely in self-defence, they may inject little or no venom. The severity of a venomous bite is determined directly by how much and how deep the venom has been injected.

Furthermore, it's not uncommon for back-fanged snakes such as the boomslang to deliver dry bites, as their fangs may not make contact during a bite, being so far back in their mouths.

Must a boomslang bite you on a digit to deliver its venom?

It's often said that the reason why so few people are envenomated by boomslangs (*Dispholidus typus*) is because they are back fanged and so their mouths cannot open wide enough for the fangs, which are positioned far back in the mouth, to come into contact with your skin. That's why you can, apparently, only become envenomated if the boomslang is able to bite you on a small, exposed or thin part of your body, like an ear, lip or little finger or toe. Balderdash!

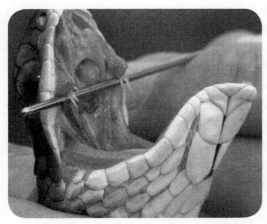

Boomslang showing the position of the back fangs.

A boomslang is in fact able to open its mouth very wide – nearly 180 degrees. Also, the fangs are not positioned way, way back in the furthest recesses of the mouth, as is the common belief; they're situated about halfway back on the upper jaw.

But as with most back-fanged snakes (such as the vine snake and the herald snake), the system for releasing venom into their venom ducts is rather primitive and not as punchy as that of front-fanged snakes. This inefficiency often requires a boomslang to bite repeatedly into its prey to ensure effective envenomation.

Usually, no sane human is going to stand still to be bitten repeatedly and boomslang envenomation in humans is indeed extremely rare; there are cases of people who have been bitten by a boomslang and who have not been envenomated (thus, a dry bite – also see the previous entry).

SNAKES: COBRAS

Why do cobras have hoods?

It's a defence mechanism used when they sense danger, in an effort to make themselves appear larger and more intimidating. Some cobras are able to lift about a third of the front of their bodies off the ground. This makes the hood look even more intimidating.

Many years ago, I spent much of my time on the unspoilt Mozambican coastline, living in a completely remote, undeveloped area. I was constructing a beach resort from scratch.

When I first arrived, with little knowledge of the Portuguese language, I was intrigued by all the reports from the workers and staff of the large numbers of 'cobras' that they encountered on the property. It seemed that they only saw cobras, and little else. This concerned me in the early days – I felt some trepidation at the thought of having developed a 'beach paradise' slap bang in the middle of an unprecedented cobra infestation. With so many cobras on the lush, verdant property, the guests, it seemed, would be destined to have a far less relaxing getaway than many would have planned. However, and to my relief, I eventually learned that the Portuguese word used by the villagers and staff for any snake is 'cobra'!

Cape cobra spreading its impressive hood.

154

The word 'cobra' as we use it today in English to refer to snakes with a hood comes from the Portuguese term *cobra de capello*, meaning 'a snake with a hood'.

Tutankhamun's mask mimics a cobra's hood and also has a rearing cobra at the top.

A cobra's hood is its trademark. The iconic image of a cobra, hood extended and with the front part of its body raised menacingly off the ground, has long been a source of fascination for humans. In the ancient Egyptian culture, for example, the symbol of a cobra poised to strike was adopted as the insignia of kings and was worn on their royal headdress.

Cobras spread their hoods by using specific muscles to expand the ribs in the neck region, behind the head. As the muscles pull these ribs open and sideways, loose skin stretches tightly over the extended ribs to form the wide, intimidating hood. The next step, for full effect, is for the cobra to raise the flared hood high off the ground to enhance the frightening effect of the defensive, if not threatening, display.

It's not only cobras that use a hood as a defensive display; other species have also latched onto this trick. Their flared hoods may not be as impressive as the true cobra hood, but they serve their purpose nevertheless. Mambas, for example, also spread a hood when threatened. So do shield-nose snakes and rinkhals (which are not true cobras).

Do spitting cobras aim for the eyes?

Cobras cannot 'spit' in the true sense of the word, but actually just contract the muscles surrounding the venom glands very suddenly. This pressure causes a jet or stream of venom to be forcefully propelled forward from a canal that exits at the front of the snake's fangs. In this way, the venom can be propelled up to 1.5 m away. The term 'spitting cobra' is therefore misleading, conjuring up images of a cobra working up a proper snarlie as it prepares for action. But let's not get too technical, and just stick with them spitting.

These snakes spit only in defence, not to immobilise or kill prey (although they can bite as well, injecting venom into their prey).

Spitters aim for the eyes and hit their targets with extreme accuracy. There's even remarkable evidence that some spitters can 'track' the movement of an aggressor, predicting accurately where its eyes will be in 200 milliseconds' time, and aim for that exact spot.

Not all cobras in southern Africa are 'spitters'. Of the eight cobra species, four cannot spit, namely the Cape cobra, the snouted cobra, the forest cobra and Anchieta's cobra. The remaining four can spit. They are the black-necked, black, zebra and Mozambique spitting cobras. The fifth spitter in southern Africa is the rinkhals, but it's not a true cobra.

Venom in the eyes will cause intense burning and will ultimately lead to blindness if left untreated. However, washing venom out of the eyes immediately using copious amounts of water (even urine, if no water is available) should lead to a full recovery.

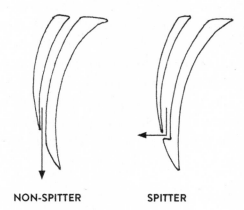

NON-SPITTER   **SPITTER**

Venom direction of a non-spitter and a spitter.

SNAKES: CONSTRICTORS

Do constrictor snakes crush or suffocate their prey to death?

There was a time when people believed that constrictors mercilessly crushed their prey to death, reducing it to a spongy sack of broken bones that would be easy for the snake to swallow. The bone-crushing theory was later replaced by one explaining that constrictors instead suffocate their prey by slowly squeezing every last breath out of it.

Both ideas are wrong. In fact, the snake kills its prey by cutting off its blood supply. The pressure applied on the body of the prey by the unrelenting, immensely powerful coils of the snake closes and shuts off the victim's blood vessels, and the heart simply isn't strong enough to keep the blood flowing through these flattened conduits.

Once the blood flow stops, the animal passes out. Death occurs shortly afterwards, as vital organs with high metabolic rates, such as the brain, heart and liver, shut down because of a lack of oxygen.

How does a constrictor know when the prey is dead?

The constrictor constantly monitors the heartbeat of its victim. The snake is able to monitor any, even the slightest, movement within its tightly encircled prey – most especially the heartbeat. Based on this signal, the constrictor either increases pressure or ceases applying pressure shortly after the heart has stopped. So, when the heart of the prey stops beating, the snake knows it is dead. And knowing precisely when it is dead saves energy.

Because the process of constriction is costly to the snake in terms of energy expenditure, it makes sense that it should constrict its prey only long enough to ensure that it is dead; anything longer would be a waste of valuable energy.

How does a constrictor breathe while constricting its prey?

When a constrictor squeezes its prey so hard that the victim's blood flow is shut off and it is unable to expand its ribs in order to breathe, surely it's a two-way street? What about the constrictor's ability to breathe?

A constrictor does not breathe by using the rib muscles and a diaphragm, like mammals do. The snake is all ribs and no diaphragm. At rest, it normally breathes air into its lungs by expanding the ribs in the upper third of its lungs. During constriction, however, it is able to 'turn on' and expand different sections of its ribcage around the lungs alternately to continue breathing, while other sections continue applying pressure. In this way the constrictor can breathe comfortably, but its victim cannot.

 SNAKES: PUFF ADDERS

How do they remain so well hidden?

Puff adders are sluggish ambush predators. Rather than constantly being on the move, searching for prey, they lie in wait for prey to find them instead.

This strategy requires stealth, patience and secrecy: the snake needs to remain undetected, not only by potential prey, but also by predators.

Puff adders have three things that count in their favour:

- ◎ **Lack of movement:** No problem for the puff adder; it can remain absolutely motionless for days (even weeks).
- ◎ **Camouflage:** The snake is a master of camouflage, blending in perfectly with its surroundings.
- ◎ **Lack of scent:** Any odours given off by a lie-and-wait ambusher could lead to its detection by potential prey and predators.

The discovery of a puff adder's lack of scent is an interesting story. Professor Graham Alexander of the Alexander Herp Lab at the University of the Witwatersrand (Wits) noticed that sniffer dogs and mongooses often blunder into or inadvertently stand on puff adders. Missing their presence due to the excellent camouflage of the snakes is one thing. But missing their scent completely is quite another. 'What if they're odourless?' he wondered.

And so the seeds were planted for a research project.

Using a team of four dogs and five meerkats (from the Montecasino Bird Gardens in Johannesburg), which were trained to detect and scent-match odour samples of snakes, Ashadee Kay-Miller, a post-graduate student in Alexander's lab, discovered in 2015 that while the sniffer team could easily, accurately and consistently identify the scents of other snake species, they were stumped when it came to nailing the puff adder scent – they simply could not smell a puff adder. Captive African elephants – which have more smell receptors than any other mammal, including dogs – were also recruited to do the puff adder sniff test – and also failed.

It was a remarkable discovery. The puff adder is the first (and at this stage the only) land vertebrate known to be scentless. The phenomenon is called chemical crypsis. The notion that a live animal could exist entirely without any semblance of scent was previously thought impossible – anything that lives and breathes must surely give off some odour owing to metabolism.

What was previously thought would be a huge, albeit hypothetical, advantage for a lie-and-wait predator was now known to be real – thanks to the puff adder and the enquiring minds of an intrepid team at a South African university.

Will a puff adder bite if you step on it?

Puff adders are sluggish snakes. As ambush hunters, they don't necessarily move away from approaching humans, as other snakes will. Instead, they stay put, relying on their supreme camouflage (and chemical crypsis – see previous entry) to remain undetected. Yet many people believe that it's this failure to move away that inevitably results in them being stepped on, more so than any other snake. And by (illogical) deduction, it's therefore thought that more people are bitten by puff adders than any other snake, which explains why the notorious title of being the most dangerous snake in South Africa was bestowed on them. (But see a previous entry that debunks this myth.)

Again, the research team from the Alexander Herp Lab at Wits came up with a game-changer. The team was tracking puff adders fitted with radio transmitters in the Dinokeng Reserve north of Pretoria. Lying motionless in their natural environment, these snakes are very difficult to spot, almost impossible sometimes, even when they're in the grass right in front of you. No one knows this better than the Wits researchers, who often inadvertently stood on the puff adders while looking for them!

But here's the thing. When the snakes were stepped on, they didn't bite. They didn't even *try* to bite. Nor did they hiss. They just remained motionless, as if cast in stone.

Intrigued, the team set out to verify this odd behaviour, which flies in the face of 'common knowledge' that puff adders will summarily bite if stepped on.

Armed with a rock-filled gumboot suspended from the end of a broomstick, they simulated stepping on or near puff adders. The snakes remained motionless and unresponsive when 'stepped' on like this while they were at rest. However, they were more likely to strike at the threatening gumboot while they were on the move.

So, myth debunked! It is not a certainty that stepping on a puff adder will result in being bitten.

Do puff adders strike backwards or eat their way out of their mothers?

The answer to this question is no on both scores. Puff adders strike fast, but not backwards. Apart from being physiologically incapable of performing such a feat, I can't help but wonder what would prompt such a 'reverse attack'. The puff adder doesn't have eyes in the back of its head, so what would it be striking at in the first place?

It is also commonly believed that puff adder babies eat their way out of their mothers. But this, too, is a myth. Puff adders give 'birth' to large litters (up to 80) of young. Like all reptiles, puff adders produce eggs, but the young snakes develop and hatch from their eggs while still inside the mother, before they emerge from her (they're ovoviviparous).

🐢 TORTOISES

Can you tell a tortoise's age by counting the rings on their shells?

Isn't it funny how often, when people find a tortoise in the bush, they will immediately examine it to determine two things: its sex – by examining its plastron (the bottom shell surface) – and its age – by counting the growth rings on its scutes (the hard scales or separate plates that make up the shell of a tortoise). After successful analysis of the unfortunate creature, the results are pronounced with a confident statement such as 'It's a 15-year-old female!' But accurately determining the age of a tortoise by counting its growth rings (called annuli) is a popular misconception, presumably derived from the comparison with growth rings of trees that denote their age.

When it comes to tortoises, it's not as simple as that. You see, the rings reflect growth spurts, not seasons or years. Perhaps adding to the erroneous belief is the fact that the rings are called annuli (singular: annulus), suggesting a ring forms annually (every year). But actually the word 'annulus' means 'a ring-shaped object', from the misspelling of the Latin word *anulus*, meaning 'little ring'.

So, while it may be true to assume that each year holds a summer feast and a winter famine, this could happen only in a world where the tortoise lived in a perfectly optimal environment throughout its life. Naturally, this is not the case: rainfall, the availability of food and water within a single season, injury, disease, stress, trauma, even egg-laying in females, and a host of other factors can influence the size or development of the rings on the scute of a tortoise. Some tortoises also have 'false rings', which don't form completely around the scute.

In a perfect world, each thick ring and the thinner ring beside it would represent one year of growth. But it doesn't work like that. Bear in mind that it's not inconceivable for a tortoise with, say, 30 rings to be anything from 10 to 50 years old. Leopard tortoises (*Stigmochelys pardalis*) can live for 100 years.

By the way, the easiest way to determine the sex of a tortoise is indeed to take a look at the plastron. If the plastron is flat, it's most likely a female. If the plastron is concave, or indented, it is most likely a male (the concave plastron of a male makes it easier for him to 'fit' onto a female when mounting her during mating).

Do tortoises die when they've 'peed' after being picked up during the dry season?

Tortoises build up a store of water in their bodies during the wet season, when water is readily available, as a reserve that they can rely on during the dry season. The liquid is stored in a sac in the rear end of the body, called the cloacal bursa. Apparently, females also use this water to moisten and soften hard sand so that they can dig a hole in which to lay eggs.

When a tortoise is picked up, it often discharges this liquid copiously as a defence mechanism, hoping to deter its assailant. Sadly, this is usually accompanied by peals of laughter from the onlookers, as the handler stands exaggeratedly bent forward and with arms stretched out to prevent a drenching by the terrified tortoise. But it's no joke.

With its water reserve now lessened or spent, the animal is not fully equipped to cover large distances in search of replenishment, since very little or no water may be freely available until the onset of the next rains.

I'm told by many that it's a 'death sentence' and that tortoises die as a result of irresponsibly being picked up in the dry season. But I've often thought about the severity of this statement. Surely tortoises are more resilient than that? Are they not often harassed or knocked about by predators or other animals in the wild? (I've seen baboons having a sports day with an unfortunate leopard tortoise – a combination of bowls, soccer and volleyball!)

Are they at risk of dying because they've released their water reserve in self-defence? Females that moisten sand in this way so that they can lay their eggs in autumn don't die, do they? To me it seems implausible that a tortoise would have only one shot at self-defence and then die.

So, is a tortoise's water reserve depleted when it's picked up? Yes. Will the tortoise die as a direct result? Unlikely. But I nonetheless firmly advocate that tortoises should be picked up only as a very last resort, and I'm happy to know that many people nowadays would not even pick a tortoise up when it's crossing a road and move it to safety, but would rather park nearby and warn oncoming traffic of its plight.

Why should you never pick up a tortoise?

I've seen tortoises being handled ham-handedly (try saying that fast!) by a field guide eager to please or educate youngsters or tourists – usually with the best of intentions. But unlike most other creatures that can growl, bite, struggle, grimace or whine, or have some other way of showing their discomfort at being handled, tortoises have no visible means of expression. Consequently, the handler is unable to detect the fear, distress or anguish that the tortoise may be experiencing after it has retreated tightly into its shell. Withdrawing into the shell in itself could be construed as a display of fear – any animal that takes specific action to hide or suddenly protect itself from imminent danger is most likely feeling threatened and expressing a stress reaction.

Turning a tortoise upside down is just as bad, and may cause the animal severe stress. This is usually done unceremoniously to demonstrate the concave plastron (bottom shell of the tortoise). It seems likely that the only time a tortoise would ever find itself upside down in nature would be after falling down a steep incline or while something is trying to eat it. Also, in some tortoise species, males in combat will actually try to flip their rivals onto their backs in a show of ultimate defeat. Tortoises are usually able to right themselves again, but not without some difficulty. And if they're unable to right themselves, they'll die a lingering death due to exposure.

It's been suggested that wild tortoises experience immense stress levels (likened to utter terror in humans) when being handled and that this state may take hours to normalise. Very few people seem to be aware of this.

So, is it really worth picking up a tortoise, even if the intention was to educate someone or engender a greater respect and understanding for these affable creatures in them? Let your conscience decide!

Part 4

FISH

SHARKS

Can sharks smell a drop of blood in the water from kilometres away?

There's a common belief that sharks have the uncanny ability to smell blood from kilometres away. As a means of comparison, they're supposed to be able to smell one drop of blood that's been diluted into an Olympic-sized swimming pool. This simply isn't true, yet many people won't even go near the ocean when they have a recent cut or scratch on their bodies.

Sharks 'smell' the water through two nostrils, called nares, situated under their snouts. These nares are dedicated entirely to smelling, not breathing. Water is drawn in through the nares into nasal sacs that contain sensory cells. Here the water is analysed for 'smells' that may match the scent of prey or a potential mate.

There are around 500 species of shark in the world. In most, the sense of smell is average, but in some, it is remarkably well developed. But none can smell blood from kilometres away. In fact, research shows that at best, some sharks might be able to sniff out fractional amounts of substances from about 400 m away.

When an enticing scent has been detected and the shark decides to follow up, it starts to swim towards the source. Its natural swimming action causes its head to sweep from side to side. This movement helps to pinpoint the exact source of the smell. The mechanism is so sensitive that the shark can determine whether a stronger signal is being registered in the left or the right nostril as the head moves, and so set a course directly towards the target.

Do sharks go into a feeding frenzy when they smell human blood?

No, it's hogwash – although it does make for entertaining movies.

As humans aren't a shark's natural prey, the chances are that sharks don't know that it's human blood that they're smelling. There's no connection for a shark between humans and human blood – it doesn't know what either of these are. Sharks also won't home in on someone who's started bleeding while in the water (for whatever reason).

Human blood does not have some sort of magical composition that will allow its molecules to spread (and be detected) instantly over a vast area. The only way that the blood scent can be dispersed from its source is by movements of water currents. It's the motion of the ocean that determines in which direction, how far or how fast a blood scent will be carried – and it may be towards *or* away from a shark.

Although the smell of mammalian blood is not 'irresistible' to sharks, they will readily detect its presence and will probably investigate it – sharks are curious by nature. But mammal blood is most certainly not at the top of their list when it comes to feeding preferences. Tests have shown that sharks are more attracted by the smell of fish blood (or perhaps the blood of marine mammals such as seals) than they are to the smell of cow's blood. Since their sense of smell is eminently better developed than their eyesight, however, they may well investigate the source of any smell that could possibly lead to a meal, including mammalian blood.

The smell of human blood also doesn't cause sharks to go into a frenzy, as is often said. I've seen a video of a diver proving this point rather dramatically. While surrounded underwater by sharks and kneeling on the seabed, he used a knife to deliberately inflict deep cuts on his arm, which bled profusely in the presence of the circling blacktip sharks. They paid absolutely no attention to the diver or the blood pouring freely from the lacerations on his arm.

Are menstruating women targets for shark attacks?

This is another myth. There is no positive evidence whatsoever that menstruation is linked to or increases the risk of a shark attack.

As for menstruating women being an obvious target for shark attacks, records of humans bitten by sharks (since the 1500s) show that 93% of the attacks involved men. This does not mean that sharks prefer biting men to women. It's simply a manifestation of the fact that men are more likely to be bitten by a shark because historically, men have participated in marine activities much more than women have. However, recent data show that more women are now involved in shark attacks, probably because of their increased participation in marine sports and activities.

Why do sharks attack humans if they're not part of the shark's natural diet?

There's not one definitive reason for such attacks, but we do know that sharks do not habitually target humans for consumption. In fact, drone footage shows how often humans are investigated by sharks without them even being aware of the threat.

A number of theories have been proposed for why sharks attack humans, the most popular being that it's a case of 'mistaken identity'. It's thought that humans, especially when bobbing around or swimming on the surface, resemble the natural prey of a shark. Viewed from below, the silhouette of a surfer paddling on a surfboard bears a strong similarity to a floundering seal. No surprises, then, that over 60% of shark attacks involve surfers or people participating in board sports.

There's also the 'bump-and-bite' theory. Sharks are known to be very curious about any object that they encounter in the water and they will usually investigate to see if it's edible. They'll circle it, then nudge or bump it with their snout, then 'mouth' or bite it to find out what it tastes like. Unfortunately, humans almost always fare badly against a shark nibble: we're fragile and composed of soft tissue with an extensive blood supply near the body surface. When a curious shark uses its mouth to taste-test us, the formidable array of teeth is almost certain to cause catastrophic, if not fatal, damage through uncontrollable bleeding.

The top three shark species responsible for inflicting serious injuries or death on humans are great whites, tiger sharks and bull sharks (also known as Zambezi sharks), but the massive terror humans associate with sharks is largely unfounded. Once again Hollywood has played the biggest part in encouraging this terror by portraying sharks as deadly man-eaters that will not hesitate to violently kill any living thing that crosses their path.

Worldwide, around 70 unprovoked shark attacks occur every year, with about 10 being fatal. To put this in perspective, coconuts falling on people's heads account for 150 deaths annually, and more people are killed by mosquitoes in a day than have been killed by sharks in a century. You have a 1 in 3.7 million chance of being killed by a shark – your chances of being struck by lightning are greater. (I know of someone who's actually been struck by lightning twice, but even more bizarre is that his name is Rod!)

Do sharks die if they stop swimming?

Some species need to swim or they'll die, but for most this is not the case.

In this case, 'die' means 'drown'. It may seem strange that a fish can drown, but drowning is simply suffocation underwater due to a lack of oxygen. Sharks breathe by using their gills to extract dissolved oxygen in the water as it flows over the gills. If no water flows over the gills, there's no oxygen to extract, and so death by suffocation will follow.

Some sharks can stop swimming whenever they want. Indeed, many benthic (bottom-dwelling) sharks live a sedentary lifestyle, hiding under rocks, in crevices or in the sand on the ocean floor. Other species, like the pelagic (open-water) sharks, need to keep moving in order to keep breathing. It all depends on the shark's breathing mechanism.

○ **Ram breathers:** Pelagic sharks such as great whites, hammerheads, makos and whale sharks are obligate ram breathers – they must swim at a certain speed, with their mouths open, to 'ram' a constant flow of water over their gills. The faster they swim, the more water flows over the gills, and the more oxygen they're able to absorb. The reverse is also true, which means that if they stop swimming or go too slow, there's not enough water flowing over the gills, and so not enough oxygen. So for them it's swim or die! Because they're active all the time, pelagic sharks are usually found in the upper, more oxygenated water columns of the oceans.

○ **Buccal pumping:** Other species, including nurse sharks (the ragged-tooth shark is a nurse shark), use a mechanism called buccal pumping. When motionless, they use their cheek muscles to actively 'inhale' water, forcing it out again over the gills for oxygen absorption. They don't need to keep swimming actively to ventilate their gills. It's just as well, since some sharks spend their lives slouching around on or near the bottom, and can sometimes stay motionless for days on end thanks to buccal pumping.

○ **Combination of ram breathing and buccal pumping:** The majority of sharks (raggies included) use both buccal pumping and ram ventilation to breathe, depending on whether they're actively swimming or not. Either way, they're able to breathe by using the most suitable breathing mechanism for the circumstances.

Skates and rays (and some shark species) that live on the ocean bed or bury themselves in sand can't suck in water through their mouths, so they use spiracles to breathe. Spiracles are paired openings between the eyes and the gill slits that draw water in, over the gills, and let it flow out again, allowing the bottom dwellers to breathe.

How far upstream do Zambezi sharks go?

Zambesi sharks are also known as bull sharks. They occur worldwide in warm waters along coasts and in estuaries and rivers. They can change their body chemistry to enable them to live in either fresh water or in the ocean because of specialised organs that allow them to regulate the salt content of their bodies.

The advantage of their ability to adapt to freshwater habitats is that they have less competition here from sharks that cannot contend with a freshwater environment. Furthermore, Zambezi sharks produce their young in fresh water, where their survival rate is higher than in the ocean.

In South Africa, Zambezi sharks have often been found over 10 kilometres upstream in rivers. There is also a report of a bull shark that travelled all the way to Alton, Illinois up the Mississippi River – 1 100 km inland!

Part 5

ARTHROPODS

ANTLIONS

When do they poo?

The funnel-shaped pits found in sand (usually in rain shadows) are made by antlion larvae. The larva moves backwards in the sand in a circular motion, flicking sand out of the pit with its head. This action creates a steep-sided, cone-shaped pit, perfect for trapping unsuspecting prey, such as ants. The larva positions itself secretively under the sand in the centre of the cone and then the waiting game begins. It's all about patience, though. It may take weeks, months or even a year for unsuspecting prey to blunder into the trap.

Antlion larva (left): Note its large sickle-shaped, pincer-like jaws.
Antlion pit traps (right).

When prey does stumble into the pitfall trap and scrambles desperately to fight its way up and out, its struggling alerts the antlion larva, dug in and ready for battle. It instantly springs into action (no surprises here – I'd also be thrilled after waiting for a year). The larva attacks mercilessly from the bottom of the pit by bombarding the prey with an incessant barrage of well-aimed sand particles. Not only does this 'shock-and-awe' onslaught impede the prey's frantic escape attempts, it also causes a mini avalanche that drags the victim down to the bottom of the cone . . . into the waiting jaws of death.

The larva seizes the prey with its large sickle-shaped, pincer-like jaws and injects enzymes into it to begin digesting the soft parts of the prey. After sucking out the digested contents through the hollow pincers (they inject *and* suck), it shovels the carcass out of the pit, resets the pit and goes back into the ambush . . . waiting in ant-icipation.

But any meal is accompanied by a pressing need – to poo. It's a problem in this case. Living in such a concentrated area, the antlion could give away its secretive presence through odours emanating from its pit. And ants have a keen sense of smell, so pooing in the pit is positively prohibited. Antlions are, well, anal about this. So much so that in order to negate odours, the antlion's anus is completely sealed off with skin, as is its mouth. The antlion overcomes the problem by storing waste products in its sealed rectum – for up to three years. When it sheds its skin, the excreta is left behind too, compelling the antlion to construct a new, odourless funnel trap.

In a silky, sandy cocoon, the larva pupates underground into a large winged adult (superficially resembling a dragonfly). Adults are clumsy, flapping fliers and are often attracted to light.

BUTTERFLIES

How do they taste what they eat?

It makes sense to think that most creatures taste their food with their mouths, because it's where food is eaten. Humans and other mammals, for example, use their tongues to taste.

But butterflies don't have tongues. Broadly speaking, their 'mouthparts' consist of a proboscis. It's curled up under the head and is not much more than a simple straw used to suck up sap, fruit juices, dissolved minerals and liquid nectar, a butterfly's main source of food. There's no biting or chewing required at all.

Although the proboscis does not have any taste receptors, as would normally be associated with a tongue, butterflies do have taste buds . . . on their feet. Researchers discovered in the late 19th century that these chemoreceptors sit on their feet; before that, everyone just assumed that butterflies tasted with their antennae or palpi, parts of their mouthparts. After all, since humans and most other mammals taste with their tongues, something similar must be the case in butterflies, the reasoning went.

When a butterfly lands on a plant, it uses something called contact chemoreception to determine whether its feet are standing in or on something sweet, sour, salty or bitter. Chemicals in the region around the butterfly's feet come into contact with the receptors; this process triggers information about the nature and taste of the chemicals to be sent to the brain. So, butterflies use their feet to make sense of chemicals, just as we use our tongues to taste food.

The chemoreceptors in their feet not only help to detect food, but are also used for choosing a mate or identifying a suitable host plant on which to lay eggs. Flitting around from leaf to leaf for taste-tip testing is no frivolous task. The female has to find an appropriate plant on which to lay her eggs, because when the eggs hatch, the caterpillars need an excellent – and non-toxic – source of food ('preselected' by the mother) so that they can immediately begin to feed to support their next step of development, during which they will encase themselves in a cocoon.

Why do butterflies congregate on mud puddles or fresh dung?

We often see groups of butterflies bunched together on the ground in a dazzling display, usually on wet sand around pools of water or mud, or on fresh animal dung. It's called 'puddling'.

Puddling is usually performed by male butterflies. They're in search of vital nutrients such as amino acids and minerals, especially sodium, which is in short supply in their nectar diet. (Sodium is what makes salt salty.) As a result, they're attracted to moist sand, dung and even carrion for a shot of sodium.

For male butterflies, sodium is a necessary ingredient for healthy sperm and successful mating. It's been shown that males on a 'sodium high' are more energetic and mate more successfully than males on a diet of only water. Sodium is also incorporated into their sperm and transferred to the females when mating. This may also help to bolster the viability of the eggs, as sodium has been shown to have a role in muscle and neural development in some butterflies.

Next time a butterfly delicately alights on your skin, don't think it's because you're special – it's likely simply because you're sweaty!

Where do the millions of white butterflies on migration come from – and where do they go?

In the central, northern and eastern parts of South Africa, it's a prodigious sight in midsummer to see a stream of small white butterflies flying in seemingly endless waves across the landscape. Like drifts of snow, they are all flying north to north-east. But where do they come from? And where are they headed?

It's a butterfly called the brown-veined white (*Belenois aurota*, also called pioneer caper whites). In December and January, they gather in their millions to migrate from the drier south-western areas to the wetter north-eastern areas of the country. It is a feast not only for the eyes but also for anything that preys on butterflies.

They fly by day and sleep in their masses at night, on grass stems or in trees, temporarily transforming their roosts into a surreal show of white. Journeys can vary from hundreds to thousands of kilometres, depending on how much prevailing winds help.

Although widespread beyond our borders, the core population in South Africa originates in the Kalahari region, where females lay their eggs on a number of larval host plants, notably shepherd's trees (*Boscia* species). In extremely favourable environmental conditions, their numbers swell in a population explosion that exceeds the food available in the area. This triggers their genetically preprogrammed mass migration to greener pastures, with eggs also being laid along the way. Numbers vary from year to year.

Since they don't come back to their point of origin (some may even meet a watery demise in the Indian Ocean off Mozambique), the journey should perhaps be seen as an emigration rather than a migration.

The concern that the mass flight of brown-veined whites could lead to agricultural disruption is completely unfounded. The adult butterflies don't eat plants and the caterpillars feed mainly on plants from the caper family. They don't cause any damage to urban gardens either or transmit disease. Enjoy them – it's a marvellous display!

CATERPILLARS

Are caterpillars worms?

No, worms don't have legs, arms or true eyes, and worms don't transform into insects. Caterpillars, in contrast, are the larval stage of moths or butterflies.

Caterpillars, like other arthropods, have a tough outer body covering, whereas worms, such as earthworms, have a segmented body with a soft, moist outer layer.

Are the hairs on caterpillars dangerous?

They can be. Caterpillars come in a fascinating variety of forms and colours. Some have eye spots, gaudy colours and even long, spine-like appendages. Since they are pretty much helpless, not being able to fly or run away from predators, they often use other, more sinister forms of defence. Most notable of these are hairs, called setae, that rub off on contact.

When the setae of some caterpillars get stuck in or even touch human skin, they can cause a rash, pain, itching, burning, blistering, swelling and even anaphylactic shock. Some caterpillars have hollow, quill-like setae attached to venom sacs. When these hairs are touched, they penetrate the skin, releasing venom. It's not uncommon to accidentally encounter setae by brushing up against a caterpillar in the bush or while gardening. There have even been reports of setae being blown by a breeze onto a person's skin or clothing, or into their eyes.

The hairs can be minute, proving difficult to remove from the skin, even when using tweezers. One way of extracting them is to carefully put a plaster or tape sticky side down on the affected area and then gently remove it, hopefully with the offending setae stuck to it.

Even though most caterpillars are not harmful, it's best not to pick up or even touch any caterpillar, especially if they're hairy.

 CENTIPEDES

Can they bite?

Centipedes are fascinating creatures that have been around for a long time – giant centipedes roamed the Earth 300 million years ago, making them among the oldest terrestrial arthrodpods.

Most people are terrified of them, and great consternation ensues when a centipede makes an appearance – and they are promptly dispatched, to everyone's great relief. They can indeed bite, although it's uncommon. But should you be unlucky enough to be bitten, fear not, for you won't die.

For some reason, people find a creature with a large number of legs or appendages scary. (Some people won't even eat anything with more than four legs!) With their bright colours and many legs, centipedes are prime candidates for instilling terror – and rightly so, as bright, contrasting colours (aposematic colouration) serve as a warning to would-be attackers.

The head has a long pair of antennae that are used more for hearing than touch. On either side of the head are two legs that have been modified into pincers. They contain venom glands. These sharp, hollow pincers are used to inject venom into their prey. A bite to a human may result in a painful swelling, but it's not life-threatening.

Centipedes can have between 15 and 170 body segments, with one pair of legs on each (millipedes have two pairs per segment – see a later entry). The last pair of legs are also prominent: thick, elongated and tipped with spines. Since they're frequently a different colour from the rest of the body, it's often incorrectly assumed that these formidable-looking structures are the 'stingers'. However, these tail feelers may in fact be used as anchoring claws or for holding on to prey.

Mating is a heartless affair. The male simply deposits a spermatophore (a capsule containing sperm) near the female's genital opening, and leaves. The sperm find their own way into the female. The female constructs a brood chamber in rotting plant matter, lays up to 60 eggs and then coils up around them to form a protective basket with her legs. She'll care for them in this way for several months until they hatch and moult. If severely threatened during this brood period, a female will rather eat her own brood than deliver them to an enemy. It makes sense: if the loss is certain, why sacrifice the protein to another when you can benefit from it yourself?

Centipedes prey on almost anything they can catch and overpower: termites, grasshoppers, cockroaches, crickets, scorpions and spiders. Some have even learned to open the doors of trapdoor spiders: so much so that some trapdoor spiders may have developed armoured plates on their abdomens to protect themselves from the centipede raiders.

When preyed upon themselves, they'll use their venom in defence. But they can also shed their legs to free themselves from a predator's grip. The lost legs are regenerated as they moult.

In South Africa we have a small brown snake with a blackish head that feeds exclusively on centipedes. In fact, it's (not very creatively) called the black-headed centipede eater. Only around 30 cm long, it is back fanged and mildly venomous. After seizing a centipede, it chews along the body of its prey until it is subdued and then swallows the centipede head first. The venom of centipede eaters is harmless to humans.

CITRONELLA CANDLES

Do they really work?

Citronella oil is an essential oil processed from a type of grass native to tropical Asia, where it is grown commercially for use in soaps, candles and insect repellents. The grass looks very much like the culinary favourite lemongrass; in fact, the two grasses are closely related.

Citronella does have a function in repelling mosquitoes. It's supposed to work not by repelling as such, but rather by masking the odours of humans that mosquitoes find attractive. To be effective, the oil has to evaporate (which is why it needs to be heated), giving off a 'haze' mosquitoes find, well, repellent. But it evaporates quickly and its beneficial effects are short-lived.

When delivered in a burning candle, the evaporating essential oil may well have a slight repellent effect on mosquitoes, but it's possible that they could also be scared off simply by the smoke from the burning wax and wick, and not necessarily the citronella additive. Perhaps the smell emitted by the candle is much more comforting to us than repellent to mossies . . . Besides, mossies are low fliers and the heat of the flame causes the smoke and chemical to rise up and away from the mosquito zone. And if there's a breeze, then the effectiveness of the already minute citronella concentrate is almost entirely diluted, significantly negating any repellent effect.

Since citronella oil is plant based and considered safe for humans when used in small quantities, it is among the most widely advertised natural repellents on the market today.

Is it all hype? You decide.

CLICK BEETLES

How do they flick and click?

If a click beetle lands on its back with its legs in the air, it is unable to get up because its legs can't reach the ground. But it has a nifty solution should it find itself in this unfortunate situation: it simply flicks itself into the air so that it can come down again, hopefully landing with the right side down this time. If not, it will try again. And again. Click, click, click.

But the jolt is no ordinary flick. It's a remarkable action that seems entirely disproportionate to the simple result required. The thorax and abdomen of a click beetle can hinge up and down by about 45 degrees. By harnessing the energy generated by employing a complex mechanism of pegs, knobs, levers, grooves, muscles and elasticity, the click beetle 'locks and loads', like a spring. Then, suddenly, it unleashes an explosive upward force with a loud 'click!' The jolt can hurl the beetle many times more than its own body length up into the air.

When a spacecraft is launched, astronauts experience an acceleration of about 3g. When a click beetle launches, its head accelerates at 380g. That's almost 130 times more than the G-force experienced by astronauts.

Although the click beetle uses this trick to right itself when it is upside down, the most important function of the powerful mechanism is probably as a survival strategy to escape from the jaws or beaks of predators. Crackling bites that smash into your palate at 380g must come as a real shock . . .

DEATH'S HEAD HAWKMOTHS

Why are they known as masters of deceit?

Humans have always had an intriguing if not morbid fascination with death's-head hawkmoths. The distinctive and amazingly realistic skull pattern on the thorax of these moths has long been associated with the supernatural.

The name of the species, which is found throughout southern Africa, is *Acherontia atropos*. The genus name *Acherontia* comes from the river Archeron, the mythological pathway leading to Hades, and *atropos* refers to the goddess of fate and destiny with that name. The moths have even featured in movies and books such as *The Silence of the Lambs*, Bram Stoker's *Dracula* and *Death with Interruptions*. Scary stuff.

Death's-head hawkmoth (left): Note the skull-like marking on the thorax.
Death's-head hawkmoth caterpillar (right).

One of the three species of death's-head hawkmoth is widespread throughout southern Africa. It's a large moth with a wingspan of over

100 mm, and has the streamlined, triangular wings when at rest that are characteristic of all hawkmoths. (The caterpillars are striking too: they have a short upright horn at the back and often sport outrageous colouration or 'eyespots' that frighten their predators.)

But death's-head hawkmoths are fascinating not only because of the formidable-looking skull-like marking on their thorax, but also because of their remarkable anti-bee weapon, which allows them to infiltrate a hive and feed on honey. This weapon is not physical armour or a chemical that protects them against bee-stings, but rather an immobilising sound.

This sound is nothing more than air-generated squeaking. The remarkable thing is that the moth swallows air into its stomach (insects don't have lungs) and then forces it out again through its proboscis as a squeaking sound. It sounds exactly like the whistling sound a queen bee produces, and when worker bees hear this sound, they 'freeze'.

So, with swallows and whistles, the relatively massive moth (compared with the size of the bees) enters the nest with impunity, the workers convinced that it's their queen, to raid honey without any fear of reprisal from the normally protective workers.

EARWIGS

Do earwigs crawl into your ears?

Well, they could, as any small insect could. But it's not their primary thing.

Ask most people what an earwig actually looks like and they probably wouldn't be able to tell you. Yet terrifying stories abound of how earwigs crawl into your ear, lay their eggs in your ear canal and then eat your brain.

Thankfully earwigs don't specialise in this horrific practice, especially as part of their life cycle. They're small insects with imposing forceps-like pincers protruding from their behinds. They feed on plants, not brains, and while they technically can bite, they rarely do so upon being handled. Should they get a grip on your skin with their pincers, they may well pinch tightly enough to puncture the skin, but with few to no side effects, seeing that they're not venomous.

Earwig with fearsome pincers.

LIGHT

Why are insects attracted to light?

Only some of the insects found around lights are actually *attracted* to the light – like a moth drawn to a flame. (But some, such as cockroaches, prefer to stay well out of the limelight.)

Most nocturnal insects buzzing around a light were simply making their way somewhere using a method that has evolved over millions of years – namely, navigating by the light given off by a bright celestial body – to ensure that they don't fly in a random, directionless path. And then they ended up around a lamp . . .

Flying insects fixate on the moon or a bright star at night, and keeping that light beam at a constant angle to their direction of flight, they set off. Because the light source is so far away, the angle remains essentially constant, providing the insect with a straight flight path.

But when it nears a brighter, artificial light and fixates on that instead to direct its course, the chosen flight angle must change as the insect approaches the light. The artificial light sends beams in all directions, and to keep the angle of the beam constant, the insect is forced into an ever-decreasing spiral, getting closer and closer to the light, until it eventually reaches the source.

When the insect reaches the light, the surrounding area is now extremely bright, which prompts some nocturnal insects to go into 'daylight mode': sleep. That's why you'll often see insects sitting motionless in a lit-up area. Daytime insects react the opposite way: they're tricked into a flurry of activity around the light. Either way, there are a lot of insects buzzing around lights at night.

Are coloured light bulbs less attractive to insects?

Yes, but only some colours have this effect.

It's all got to do with wavelength. In general, the colour receptors in insects' eyes are less receptive to shorter wavelengths, such as red, orange and yellow light. In line with this, research shows that light-emitting diode bulbs (modern energy-saving bulbs commonly known as LEDs) that produce a yellow or orange hue attract insects least, while traditional incandescent (heat-generating) bulbs and those that emit a cool-looking blue hue attract the most insects.

Insects are attracted to blue light, and even more so to ultraviolet (UV) light (that's how bug zappers work). Some insects are attuned to UV light because it helps them to find where the pollen is in certain flowers that have UV-absorbing pigments. Bug zappers work by using UV light to attract insects onto an electrified grid that shocks any insect landing on it, with a satisfying sizzle.

But if you've installed a bug zapper to keep mossies at bay, you've wasted your money: mosquitoes are not attracted to UV light.

MILLIPEDES

Are they dangerous?

It depends on who you are. If you're a human, they probably won't cause you much harm. If you're an insect, they can kill you.

Millipedes are slow-moving animals, with no outwardly apparent defence mechanisms: no powerful wings or legs with which to flee and no pincers, stingers or sharp appendages. Truth be told, they're sitting ducks, especially when they roll up on the spot into a seemingly helpless coil.

But they do have a secret weapon: chemical warfare. They make themselves unpalatable by secreting foul-smelling compounds through pores above their legs. The compounds can vary from mild irritants to potent poisons. One species can even squirt its chemical weapon from pores behind its head onto its attacker some distance away. And more often than not, they advertise this impending danger with their bright, contrasting colours, warning potential attackers to stay away.

They have a variety of noxious chemicals in their arsenal, such as iodine compounds that can cause blistering on the human skin and prussic acid (hydrogen cyanide). The cyanide gas released by millipedes can be lethal to insects. Interestingly, scientists make use of this trick: researchers collecting insects in the field are known to place millipedes in collecting jars to quickly kill insects that they have collected. When exposed to the cyanide gas, the insects die within seconds.

Like the cunning entomologists, other creatures have also learned to use the millipede's chemical defences to good effect. Wild dogs and some birds are known to harass millipedes, causing them to unleash their chemicals. The defensive millipede is then thoroughly rolled upon by the attackers in an effort to anoint themselves with an effective insect repellent – much as we would administer flea powder to a pet. Similarly, when building their nests, hornbills are known to chop up millipedes and spread them onto the mud that they use, possibly as an insect deterrent, fungicide or antibiotic.

Some creatures are immune to the effects of millipede chemicals. Certain scorpions, beetles and bugs feed only on millipedes. Larger ground-dwelling birds such as ostrich, guinea fowl and spurfowl, ibis and hornbills will also eat millipedes. Civets especially are well known as millipede munchers. So are meerkats, hedgehogs and jackal. Mongooses may rough up a millipede for some time before eating it, presumably enticing the millipede to rid itself of a load of toxins before being eaten.

Apart from their hard, armoured shell, chemical defences and their ability to roll up into a tight ball to protect their legs, some millipedes resort to another impressive defensive action when threatened. They turn onto their backs with accentuated, slithering motions, their red legs exposed and prominent. This sudden and unexpected transformation into violent, snake-like activity (aptly called 'swearing') is probably designed to shock or frighten an attacker and allows the millipedes to make a much quicker getaway than on their legs.

Millipedes are also called shongololos, from the isiZulu word *ukushonga*, which means 'to roll up or wrap'. Afrikaans speakers often call them a *duisendpoot* (thousand foot). But no millipede comes close to having a thousand legs – about 700 to 800 legs is the nearest they'll get.

There are almost 400 millipede species in South Africa. They feed mainly on plant litter, but will also eat dung and dead insects, and have even been seen feeding on animal carcasses.

Massive 'outbreaks' of millipedes can occur when temperature, moisture and food conditions are perfect. In these times areas are literally covered by millipedes, to the extent that cattle are unable to graze and railroad traffic comes to a stop because trains' wheels can't get traction on the rails.

Like centipedes, millipedes are among the oldest land animals. Some giant prehistoric millipedes were 2 m long!

MOPANE WORMS

Are they worms?

No, they're caterpillars, and caterpillars aren't worms (see an earlier entry explaining this).

Mopane worms are the larval caterpillars of a type of emperor moth (*Imbrasia belina*), which are giants among the moths of the world.

The caterpillars are large, up to 10 cm long and 1 cm thick, with striking yellow, black, orange and white bands. They're armed with short, sharp spines down the length of their entire body, each associated with tufts of fine, white hair.

Hairs, spines and bright, contrasting colours are a textbook warning to stay away. Such aposematic colouration signals danger to potential predators. When handled, the hairs and spines can cause irritation to humans. Yet mopane worms are an important source of insect protein for humans in southern Africa. They are eviscerated and then boiled, roasted or dried to remove the hairs.

Contrary to common belief, mopane moths don't lay their eggs exclusively on mopane trees, although it is their preferred host plant. They will also lay their eggs on maroela, fig and jackalberry trees. In productive seasons the eggs are laid in such numbers that the emerging caterpillars completely defoliate the trees on which they hatched. They then move on to the next tree. In this way, large tracts of vegetation available to browsing animals can be annihilated.

Mopane worms.

Caterpillars play a significant role in mopane-veld ecology. Apart from converting plant matter into bioavailable nutrients, they're heavily preyed on by birds, parasitised by certain wasps and flies, and, of course, harvested by humans – so much so that the decline in mopane worm numbers due to overutilisation by humans is a cause for concern. Thousands of tons are harvested annually. They're eaten fresh or dried, the advantage being that in the dried form, they remain preserved as a valuable food source for long periods even after the hatching season. They're then rehydrated and used in various ways, the most popular being in stews.

When ready to pupate, the caterpillars burrow into the ground. Here they overwinter, emerging the next season as an adult moth. They're among the biggest moths in South Africa, with a wingspan of around 12 cm. The moths are beautifully coloured in shades of brown, cream, red and green, with dramatic 'eyespots' on their wings, which are thought to trick potential predators into thinking they're faced with a larger, potentially dangerous creature, and so scare them away.

The moths don't have much of a life. They live for only three or four days and don't even feed (they don't have mouthparts). During this brief existence, the moths mate, the female lays her eggs and the cycle continues.

Mopane emperor moth.

MOSQUITOES

Are they the creatures that cause the most deaths in humans?

It's said that malaria, transmitted by mosquitoes, has been the cause of more deaths than all the wars in history. But although one of the types of mosquito we get in South Africa (a species in the genus *Anopheles*) transmits malaria, mosquitoes in other parts of the world also transmit viruses and parasites that cause dangerous diseases, such as yellow fever, dengue fever, West Nile fever and some forms of encephalitis. That's why it's said that mosquitoes kill more people than any other creature in the world – they are responsible for about 700 000 deaths a year, according to the World Health Organization.

Anopheles mosquitoes (the ones that transmit malaria) are easily identifiable by their posture: the body is aligned at a 45-degree angle when at rest and it has long, black-and-white stripy hind legs. Only the females transmit the parasite that causes malaria.

Both male and female mosquitoes feed on water and plant nectar, but females need a blood meal to reproduce. That's why they're equipped with long, hollow mouthparts capable of piercing skin to feed on blood. When the skin is pierced (they don't 'bite' as such), saliva is injected at the site, which causes the tell-tale, itchy bump on the skin. People react to the saliva of the same species in different ways, and different species of mosquito may have a more 'potent' saliva, causing a more severe reaction.

Why do mosquitoes make a high-pitched buzzing sound?

The characteristic buzzing whine made by mosquitoes is caused by them beating their wings up to 1 000 times per second. But it's impossible for any muscle to expand and contract at this rate, so how do they do it?

Elasticity. The wings are hinged onto elastic plates attached to the thorax. Muscles kick-start the action that causes the plates to oscillate, and so the attached wings start to 'flap'. After that only intermittent muscle action is needed to keep the oscillation going.

Thinking that a 'mosquito is a mosquito' couldn't be further from the truth. There are many different species (about 3 500 species in the world, over 800 species in Africa and around 113 species in southern Africa), and you will likely find a dozen or more species in a spot at one time. In fact, the different species share the available hosts by working in shifts – different species may bite you at different time slots between dusk and dawn.

With so many different species sharing the same area, males need to recognise females of their own species, which they do by using their sensitive feather-like feelers (antennae) to home in on the sound of their own kind, and more specifically, the sound of a female that has just had a blood meal. Since she's heavier, her 'buzz pitch' changes, signalling to the male that she is ready for mating.

Do mosquito repellents work?

I've often witnessed an outdoor gathering at night, the table or benches dotted with burning citronella candles, each one carefully placed as if to say, 'Take that, pesky mosquitoes!' At the same time, some people are wearing mossie-repellent bracelets or clip-on devices, while others have sprayed themselves with aerosols, painted themselves with 'mossie sticks' or slathered themselves in bug-deterring cream (doubling as a moisturiser). Some announce that their 'armour' is in their clothing, which has been washed in a repellent chemical. Not to mention the soundless ultrasonic devices competing with the randomly placed mossie coils. Oh, and then there are the garlic and vitamin B12 munchers, smugly convinced that they are immune . . .

Many of these products are gimmicks and marketing stunts. Citronella oil, for one, can have a slight repellent effect (see the entry on citronella oil earlier), but it's likely short-lived. Certain geranium types, sold as 'mosquito plants', are supposedly capable of repelling mosquitoes. But, sorry, they don't work. If anything, their moist, leafy darkness provides a safe haven for mosquitoes during the day.

Something that does work is a chemical known as DEET, short for diethyltoluamide (it should not be confused with DDT, a harmful chemical that was used as an insecticide in the past). DEET is safe for human use and is delivered in aerosol sprays, mists, wipes and lotions; it is often also used in 'fogging' homes against mosquitoes. It offers protection not only against mosquitoes but also against biting insects such as bugs and ticks, and is said to have a longer-lasting effect than most plant-based deterrents.

I'm certainly not proposing that you don't use any potions or lotions, but be sure to understand the distinction between malaria prevention and avoiding pesky irritation, and act accordingly. Use a repellent of your choice, but above all, cover as much exposed skin as possible with light clothing in summer. Exposure to a breeze or sleeping under a fan is also effective, as mossies are weak fliers.

Are mosquitoes more attracted to some people than others?

Mosquitoes are, in general, attracted to humans by smell rather than sight. They pick up on the carbon dioxide that we exhale (although this gas is odourless to us), lactic acid expelled through sweat on our skin and other odours drifting off our bodies. They're also prone to target people with certain blood types or higher body temperatures – mosquitoes can detect infrared radiation (heat) at a distance.

Because people produce different concentrations of odours, it follows that some people will have more distinct chemical signatures and that mosquitoes will find them more attractive. This could be the reason for some people being so-called 'mosquito magnets'.

Why do mosquitoes seem to target our feet?

Because they're smelly (see the previous entry). Besides, mosquitoes are low flyers, and feet and ankles are right in their flight path.

Mossies often bite feet because they're attracted by the odours caused by specific bacteria that colonise our feet, and the ankles, apart from being directly adjacent to the feet, are often left exposed.

Feet and ankle 'hits' are so common that this has resulted in some clever targeted marketing for yet more mossie-repelling gimmicks. There's even a product designed specifically for socks, which claims that socks washed in the repellent will remain active for nearly 10 months or up to 30 cold-water washes. The product might be pulling the wool over your eyes, though. Simply wearing socks may be enough of a physical barrier to keep your feet and ankles safe.

SCORPIONS

What makes scorpions glow under UV light?

The discovery that scorpions glow brightly under UV light came about only some 60 years ago. At the time, only a few hundred species of scorpion had been recorded. Today, however, scientists have discovered and recorded almost 2 000 scorpion species, this startling phenomenon no doubt being a major contributor to their discovery at night.

When UV light passes over a scorpion, it's almost as if it magically 'switches on' to radiate a dazzling, green-blue neon glow. It has quite an astonishing visual impact at night!

The outer layer of a scorpion's exoskeleton, the cuticle, contains an extremely thin but very tough coating called the hyaline layer.

Fluorescent compounds within this layer are able to absorb UV light and reflect it in other visible wavelengths as a green-blue glow.

These fluorescent chemicals are potent. When scorpions are preserved in a jar of alcohol, the liquid glows under UV light, too. Even more impressive is the fact that fossilised scorpions that have been embedded in rock for hundreds of millions of years also glow when exposed to UV light.

Interestingly, though, the soft cuticles of recently moulted scorpions do not glow in the dark. Scorpions need to shed their exoskeletons through moulting from time to time, as part of the growing process. Only when the new cuticle is completely dry and fully hardened will it fluoresce and glow under UV light. This implies that the chemicals that cause the fluorescence are either by-products of the hardening process or are secreted as a separate event not long after the scorpion has moulted. It's yet to be discovered which of these two mechanisms is in play.

Scorpions fluoresce under UV light.

Why do they glow in the dark?

In other words, what benefit does a scorpion derive from being visible in UV light? It's a subject that's still hotly debated, with a number of theories having been proposed.

Some ideas are that they glow under the faint UV exposure that exists at night so that they can find one another in the dark. Others propose that they glow so that they can dazzle UV-sensitive prey at night or that it's a way to protect themselves from sunlight during the day. But these are, at best, stabs in the dark.

One hypothesis that does seem to have some merit, though, is based on the observation that scorpions tend to avoid visible light (they seem to be less active on moonlit nights) in general and are not comfortable when exposed to UV light. So, the thinking is that scorpions use their entire bodies as sensors to detect faint UV signals at night. By determining just how much UV light is shining on them, they know how much of their body is exposed. Consequently, they are better able to conceal themselves. Whether to remain hidden or to expose themselves by going on a hunt then seems to depend on how much (or little) UV light their body is exposed to at the time.

But perhaps there's no reason at all why they dazzle in the dark. Perhaps it's just a random evolutionary quirk of nature?

 # SPIDERS

Can they kill you?

Many people have an undeniable fear of spiders. It's called arachnophobia (from the Greek mythological character Arachne, who was turned into a spider, and the word *phobos*, meaning 'fear'). It may have a similar origin in our heads as ophidiophobia, the fear of snakes (see page 133), but it could also be fuelled by people knowing that spiders are all around them, yet not knowing where exactly, leaving them feeling exposed to a possible bite when vulnerable, like when asleep. Or it might be that the 'legginess' of spiders is what causes so much alarm. The disproportionally long legs – eight of them, no less! – and their erratic movements seem to suggest that the creature can launch itself unpredictably in any direction. As for the idea that we are genetically programmed to avoid spiders as an ancestral survival technique, I don't buy it. If this were so, we should be programmed to avoid almost anything that can cause us harm, whether that is a scorpion, a spider or a snake, or anything else for that matter.

Whatever the reason for spiders being among the most feared creatures on Earth, let's get some perspective. Over 2 230 spider species have been identified in South Africa, yet no deaths by spider bite have been recorded in the country in the last 50 years.

All spiders have fangs and almost all spiders are venomous to some degree, although the bites of only a handful are considered as being of medical consequence.

Here's a brief overview of six of the better-known spiders in South Africa, all of which have a reputation as 'killers'.

* **Button spiders:** Firstly, button spiders are not the same as widow spiders. We don't get black widow or brown widow spiders (as they are called in the United States) here in South Africa; these are cousins of the button spiders found in southern Africa. Until recently eight species of button spider were known in Africa, but a ninth one – the Phinda button spider (*Latrodectus umbukwane*) – has recently been identified in South Africa.

  As the name suggests, the black button spider (*Latrodectus indistinctus*) is completely black and it does not have a red hourglass marking on the underside, although there may be some red on the top of the abdomen and above the spinneret.

Black button spider.

Black button spiders are considered highly venomous and potentially lethal, although there are no records over the last 50 years of anyone dying from a black button spider bite in South Africa.

Brown button spider.

Brown button spiders (*Latrodectus geometricus*) vary in colour from grey to black. Geometric markings are found on the top of the abdomen, while the bottom has a red to orange hourglass marking (finally, the red hourglass marking with which we are all so obsessed!) The giveaway identifying characteristic is the spider's brown legs, which have dark joints between the sections.

The brown button spider is considerably less venomous than the black one. Both have neurotoxic venom that causes sweating, pain, nausea, disorientation, droopy eyelids and dilated pupils.

Black and brown button spiders are found throughout most of South Africa. They build untidy, three-dimensional webs and are often seen carrying whitish egg sacs. The egg sacs of the black button spider are smooth, while those of the brown one have spiky projections.

❋ **Violin spiders:** Twelve species of this type of recluse spider occur in South Africa. They are brown to grey, have a characteristic violin shape on their thorax and may have markings on the abdomen. They are free living (meaning they don't build webs). The venom is cytotoxic, and can cause severe tissue damage and

Violin spider.

open, septic wounds if left untreated. No one has ever died from a violin spider bite in South Africa.

✳ **Sac spiders:** These spiders are light coloured – cream to reddish brown. Their dark, blackish mouthparts against the pale body are a dead giveaway when it comes to identification. They are free living, but produce silk sacs under which they hide or lay eggs. Cytotoxins in the venom can cause open, septic wounds if left untreated.

Sac spider.

✳ **Baboon spiders:** These are large, robust and intimidating spiders with a leg span of up to 15 cm. South Africa has 44 different species. Only the females live in silk-lined burrows in the ground.

Baboon spider in defensive position.

When threatened, these spiders raise their front legs dramatically, ready to strike forward to bite in self-defence. Being such hefty spiders, they have long fangs, which can deliver a painful bite. Apart from short-lived pain and discomfort, the venom has little effect on humans and symptoms clear up within a day or two.

* **Jumping spiders:** There are more than 60 different kinds of these common little spiders with their characteristic head-lamp-like eyes, which are so often seen and encountered in homes, in South Africa. None of these spiders are bigger than 2 cm across. Being so numerous and free-ranging, they often take the blame for any form of 'bite' that may have occurred in

Jumping spider.

the home. But their venom is considered harmless to humans.

Are daddy long-legs the most venomous spiders in the world?

When it comes to dangerous spiders, one of the most widely recounted fallacies is that daddy long-legs are the most venomous spiders in the world, but because their fangs are too small to penetrate our skin, they're harmless. This implies that millions of people live their entire lives moments away from a spidery death by the dreaded 'baddy' long-legs, spared only by the thickness of their skin!

Daddy long-legs spiders are common throughout South Africa, possibly the most well-known spiders around. Their venom is completely harmless. They're usually found in dark, undisturbed corners of houses and sheds, or under beds and chairs, sheltering within a tangled, untidy, three-dimensional web. When abandoned, these webs gather dust and become cobwebs (cobwebs are webs that are no longer in use).

Their legs are long, fragile and impossibly thin – they move around with an awkward rocking or shuddering motion. And it's these thin legs that often cause them to be confused with violin spiders, which are capable of a serious bite that can result in a debilitating wound if left untreated. However, the legs of violin spiders are not as thin as those of daddy long-legs. Perhaps this is how the myth of the deadly daddy long-legs arose? Nonetheless, it's unfounded. No record exists of bites (even just bites, let alone bites requiring medical treatment) from daddy long-legs anywhere in the world.

Like all other spiders, they do more good than harm by eating insects and other spiders, so there's no need, ever, to kill a daddy long-legs spider hiding in the home. Rather coax it gently into a dustpan or container and release it in the garden. You'll both feel better about this course of action . . .

Daddy long-legs spider.

Part 6

PLANTS

ACACIAS

Where have all the acacias gone?

The days of describing the silhouette on that classic African sunset photograph as that of an acacia tree are gone. That's because acacias don't exist in South Africa any longer, or in Africa for that matter. Shocked that an icon has disappeared? Fear not, it's just the name, not the tree itself.

The term *Acacia* officially became extinct from the African savanna over a decade ago, but few people know why. Surely acacias are quint-essentially African? The first type species of the genus was described in Africa by Philip Miller in 1754 (namely *Acacia scorpioides*, the scented thorn, or *lekkerruikpeul* in Afrikaans). Acacia 'thorn trees' (*doringbome* in Afrikaans) have been synonymous with Africa ever since, it can be argued.

But all of this was of little consequence at the 17th International Botanical Congress held in Melbourne in 2011, where a group of Australian botanists declared that the genus Acacia – or wattles, as they call them – is distinctly Australian and occurs only in Australia, and that the word 'acacia' can only be used to describe the hundreds of native Australian wattle species. The rest of the world, they proposed, would need to find new names for the trees previously called acacias. (Much like the argument, in a way, where the word 'champagne' 'belongs' only to the Champagne region in France or 'port' to Porto in Portugal.)

Yet the scented thorn was assigned to the genus *Acacia* 16 years *before* (then Lieutenant) James Cook arrived at Botany Bay, Australia aboard the HMS *Endeavour* in 1770. It was argued that Africa had prior claim to the name because it was recorded as such before Australia even existed, and so Australians should be renaming *their* wattle trees (to *Racosperma*) rather than Africans having to rename their thorn trees (to *Vachellia* and *Senegalia*).

But the botanists from down under countered that since most of the world's named acacias (960 out of 1 350 known species) were native to Australia, the name clearly belonged to Australia, never mind that it was first named in Africa. Besides, Australia's national floral emblem is the golden wattle (*Acacia pycnantha*).

The naming rights for acacias became a thorny issue. Long and complicated deliberations on the matter eventually swung in the favour of Australia: the right to *Acacia* was to be reserved for species native to Australia, and Africa had to use the genera *Vachellia* and *Senegalia*.

That's how science works. It's a continuous process of re-evaluation and correction to accommodate the most convincing evidence at that time. Things like naming conventions and rules change in science and, like with the renaming of so many South African bird species (still a bone of contention, sadly, with some antiquated, fossilised twitchers), we need to stop using the previous names and adapt our vocabulary to incorporate the new nomenclature.

Some of the most damaging invasive alien tree species that occur in South Africa belong to the (Australian genus) *Acacia*. They include the pearl acacia (*Acacia podalyriifolia*), the black wattle (*Acacia mearnsii*) and the Port Jackson willow (*Acacia saligna*), the most damaging invasive species in coastal south-western Cape.

 # BAOBAB TREES

How old are they?

It's not a simple exercise to determine their age, but we know it's not 6 000 years (which is, according to New Earth theorists, how old the Earth is . . .).

The age of trees can usually be determined by measuring their annual growth rings – a cross-section of concentric circles within the stem that show the amount of wood produced in a growth season. But in some years baobabs don't produce growth rings, while in others they may produce more than one. In addition, the growth rings may fade away over time. That's why researchers use carbon dating techniques instead to determine the age of these trees. But even then, the results may not be spot on. Different stems in a large baobab may be from different generations at different times on the same tree, and so can have different ages.

There's much speculation about the ages of the largest baobab trees in southern Africa. Some are boldly stated as being over 6 000 years old, although one wonders how such estimates may have been derived without modern dating techniques. According to carbon dating techniques and core sampling, it's reasonable to assume that trees with a diameter of 10 m may well be over 1 000 years old.

South Africa's two largest baobabs both stand in the Limpopo province. The Sagole Baobab, located between Tshipise and Pafuri, is considered to be South Africa's largest tree. Its stem diameter is just over 10 m and its crown spread is 38 m. Carbon dating suggests that Sagole is 1 200 years old.

The Sagole Baobab is the largest baobab tree in South Africa.

The Glencoe Baobab near Hoedspruit is the second largest. Its stem diameter is nearly 16 m (5 m more than Sagole), with a crown spread of 37 m (about the same as Sagole). Glencoe's age has been carbon dated to around 1 800 years. Even though Glencoe's stem diameter is larger and it's an older tree, it still takes second place to Sagole because its overall 'size index' (the application of a certain botanical formula) is less than that of Sagole.

A baobab tree may be over 1 000 years old, but its flowers last for only a day. The flowers bloom in the late afternoon, are pollinated by bats during the night and drop off the tree within 24 hours.

Ironically, it's our very reverence for these ancient behemoths that may ultimately lead to their demise. The oldest baobabs are becoming tourist attractions, but the trampling feet of thousands of tourists will collectively, over time, compact the soil around the tree's root system, diminishing water seepage into the soil. This reduces water uptake by the roots, which could lead to the death of the tree. Boardwalks as viewing platforms around these famous trees have been proposed as a solution.

FISH POISON

Can plants be used to poison fish?

This is indeed so – and especially true of the cork bush (*Mundulea sericea*). This plant, also aptly alled *visgif* in Afrikaans ('fish poison'), is widespread throughout Africa. A bundle of roots, bark and leaves from this plant is typically pounded, weighed down with a stone and submerged in a pond of standing water. Fish, starting with the smaller ones, will soon begin to float to the surface, swimming erratically or up-side down. They are then easily netted or caught with the bare hands.

The cork bush contains chemical compounds such as rotenoids, which diffuse into the water. Fish absorb rotenone through their gills directly into their bloodstream. This inhibits the process in which cells use oxygen to release energy, and the fish cells and tissues start to die. High concentrations of these compounds will kill not only fish but also small crocodiles!

Cork bush. It is traditionally used as a fish poison.

Is it dangerous to eat these 'poisoned' fish? There are some cases of people, who have apparently become ill after eating fish poisoned in this way. However, it is commonly accepted that cooking or drying the fish rids the flesh of any traces of the poison. Interestingly, antelope and livestock eat the bark and leaves of the cork bush without any ill effects.

Other species of plant traditionally used as fish poisons (piscicides) in South Africa include the impala lily, common tree euphorbia, umzimbeet, white pear, tamboti tree, wild syringa and fish-bean plants.

JUMPING BEANS

What are they?

The seeds of a tamboti tree, more often than not. The fruits of tamboti trees are three-lobed capsules, which burst open forcefully when ripe (such seeds are said to be dehiscent), leaving the seeds scattered on the ground under the tree.

The small grey snout moth (*Emporia melanobasis*) lays its eggs in the three-lobed tamboti fruits while they're still green and the larvae develop in a hollow inside the growing fruit segments. When the fruit segments split, the seeds fall to the ground with the larvae, now doubled over into a bow shape, inside them. Using fluid pressures in the body, they suddenly contort with enough force to cause the entire seed to 'bounce', as if by magic, sometimes hopping off the ground. Their twitching antics are performed in an effort to get out of the sun. Anyone who knows their jumping beans will tell you, just place them in the sun for a marvellous bouncy display, guaranteed to delight adults and children alike.

LEADWOOD TREES

Are there really leadwood trees that are 3 000 years old?

I'd bet that this myth stems from bush lore that says a leadwood grows for 1 000 years, takes 1 000 years to die and another 1 000 years to decompose back into the soil.

But it's not true at all. These bushveld icons are often reputed to be thousands of years old, probably because they can grow up to 20 m tall and dead trees have been known to remain standing stoically for almost a century. Specimens of long-dead trees have been known to several successive generations of farmers on a particular farm.

Carbon dating shows that they can grow to be hundreds of years old. The oldest leadwood tree examined had lived for over 1 000 years, but it's far off the reputed 3 000 years. Also, a tree of this age is the exception rather than the rule: most leadwood trees die before they attain a trunk diameter of 1 m. They grow extremely slowly, the radial growth rate being only 0.5 – 2 mm per year, depending on rainfall.

The wood is extremely heavy and dense. In fact, it sinks in water (it's called leadwood for a reason!). Its hardness makes it impervious to attacks by termites or wood borers. As a result, the wood has been overexploited in some regions for building materials, fence posts and firewood – it's revered by many in South Africa as the best of all braai woods because it burns slowly, with intense heat, and generates long-lasting, glass-hard coal (hence the name *hardekool* in Afrikaans). The wood is so hard that it was used to make implements like hoes before metal was available in Africa.

In traditional medicine, flowers of the leadwood tree are used to make cough mixture, smoke from burning leaves is used to treat colds and chest ailments, boiled root decoctions are administered for stomach pains and diarrhoea, bilharzia is treated with leaves and roots, and the white ash is used as toothpaste or mixed with water to create a whitewash paint. Some tribes believe that the spirits of their ancestors dwell in the boughs of ancient leadwoods.

It is little wonder that leadwoods are protected under the National

Forests Act today. It's illegal to damage, cut, disturb or destroy any of around 50 different species of tree on the Protected List without a specific licence granted by the Department of Environment, Forestry and Fisheries – even cutting or breaking a branch of one of these trees can lead to a hefty fine or imprisonment of three years, or both. Not that elephants pay any attention to this law . . .

 # STAPELIAS

How are these plants pollinated?

There are many more possibilities than birds and bees when it comes to plant pollinators. Plants can also be pollinated by wind, moths, butterflies, bats, beetles – or flies.

Many flowers produce sweet-smelling scents to lure insects for pollination. Some plants even try to attract *specific* insects: the more specific a plant is in attracting a certain insect, the better its chance of having pollen transported to a flower of its own species.

Stapelias (also called African starfish flowers or carrion flowers) generally don't bother with such niceties. They stink to high heaven, their foul-smelling flowers exuding the odour of rotting flesh. The strong carrion aromas are remarkably pervasive, detectable from far away, especially on hot days. Some conniving stapelias even take this 'carrion bluff' a step further . . . the colour and patterns on the flower mimic decaying animal matter and even maggots.

This entire charade is a ploy to attract their pollinator partners: flies. The putrid smell is so effective at enticing flies that they are often tricked into laying their eggs in the corona of the flower, convinced that the cache of 'dead flesh' that they've discovered will be a perfect food source for their developing larvae.

But wait, there's more. To make sure that they take the fullest advantage of an unsuspecting fly, the reproductive parts of the stapelia flower have complex structures that can trap the legs and mouthparts of flies. As the fly struggles to free itself, specialised clips containing the stapelia's pollen sacs attach to the fly. This ensures that the pollen sacs are carried to the next putrid-smelling stapelia flower, where the reproductive cycle is completed. The pollen germinates, fertilisation occurs and seeds develop. The seeds are dispersed by wind.

Giant stapelia flower.

 TAMBOTI TREES

Is it poisonous?

Tamboti trees, which grow in the warmer regions of South Africa, extending up to Tanzania, are renowned for their hard wood, used for the construction of houses and fence posts, and, most famously, in the manufacture of beautiful jewellery trinkets and furniture pieces.

The wood has a characteristic pleasant sweet smell, probably from the milky latex that it produces – which is poisonous to humans. The plant exudes this latex at a site of damage – almost as if the species has developed an innate protection against overexploitation by humans. Yet we've nonetheless found many uses for its wood.

When tamboti wood burns, it releases thick, grey, sweet-smelling smoke as a result of the latex sap being heated. Eating meat or food cooked on or exposed to this toxic smoke causes an upset stomach and diarrhoea. However, if the wood is left to burn long enough, until there is no longer any trace of smoke or smell whatsoever, excellent braai coals are produced.

My brother, Brian Coetzee, is a renowned woodcraftsman and box-maker. He'll tell you that you must take the utmost care when working with tamboti wood. He wears a facemask and goggles when crafting an object from this beautiful and sought-after wood. 'Tamboti sawdust can damage the eyes, possibly even causing blindness,' he warns, 'and it can be a severe irritant on the skin.'

African peoples place slivers of freshly cut tamboti wood with stored clothing and fabrics to repel insects and fish moths. Others harvest the poisonous latex for use as a fish poison. The latex has also been used to poison arrowheads.

Although poisonous to humans, the tamboti has always had a role in African folk medicine. The drop of latex released at the end of a leaf's stem when picked soothes toothache. When the drop is touched onto the exposed nerve, the pain is immediately numbed. The sap is also rubbed into ulcers and boils, and vapours released from boiling tamboti roots are used to cure eye infections (contrary to my brother's warnings) and relieve stomach ulcers – risky, because high dosages can cause severe organ damage. Whenever I come across the use of poisonous plants for medicinal purposes in tribal folklore, I always wonder about the trial-and-error experimentation over the ages, with horrific consequences no doubt, in attempting to perfect dosages. But that's the subject for another book . . .

Despite these hazards to humans, many animals feed with impunity on the tamboti. The leaves are browsed with great relish by kudu, nyala, bushbuck, giraffe, black rhino and elephant. Doves, spurfowl, guinea fowl and vervet monkeys eat the fruits.

WILD DAGGA

Is it a substitute for cannabis?

No. Wild dagga (*Leonotis leonurus*) is widespread throughout South Africa. It's hardiness, fast growth and striking orange-red flowers make it a popular garden plant. It also attracts bees and various species of sunbird that feed on the sweet nectar within its tubular flowers. It's part of the mint family.

I have no doubt that the hype around this plant stems from its name, wild dagga, which holds promise for some. But alas, head to head, it may disappoint.

The leaves and flowers have been smoked by the Khoikhoi for hundreds of years because of the apparent associated calming effect. They called it *dacha*. But the psychoactive effects are said to be extremely mild compared with cannabis – and wild dagga is certainly not a hallucinogenic. Apparently, the effects from smoking the plant range from mild elation to visual impairment, dizziness, light-headedness, nausea and sweating. More cons than pros, I'd think?

Wild dagga.

But there's no doubt that the primary reason for the use of wild dagga by African people through the ages is for the treatment of illnesses. Tea boiled from the leaves, roots and flowers is used to treat almost anything: fever, headaches, asthma, haemorrhoids, dysentery, coughs, itches, muscle cramps, influenza, jaundice, boils, tapeworms . . . Cattle and poultry also fall foul of doses of this 'wonder plant'. It's even used to treat bee-stings, scorpion stings and spider bites, snakebite – and to keep snakes away.

Animal trials showed that at high doses, extracts of the plant can be fatal. Scientists therefore advise that medicinal treatment using wild dagga should be administered with caution.

What's the difference between . . .

A hare and a rabbit?

Generally, hares are bigger and have proportionally longer ears and hind legs than rabbits.

South Africa has three hare species, namely the Cape hare (*Lepus capensis*), the scrub hare (*Lepus saxatilis*) and the African savanna hare (*Lepus microtis*).

There are four species of rabbit that occur here: Jameson's red rock rabbit, Smith's rock rabbit, the Natal red rock rabbit and the critically endangered riverine rabbit. The term 'critically endangered' means that they face an extremely high risk of extinction in the wild.

Male hares are called jacks and females are called jills. Jills give birth to between one and three young, called leverets. Leverets are born with their eyes and ears open, are fully furred and are ready to rock in two days. Because their young are precocious (meaning they're able to move around freely from birth and require little parental care), hares don't need to make nests for their young.

Rabbit males are called bucks and females are called does. Does of the South African species also give birth to between one and three young, called kittens. Rabbit kittens are born helpless and naked, with their ears plugged and their eyes closed. Their young are altricial (meaning that they're born in an undeveloped state and rely on parental care), which is why rabbits have protected nests lined with grass and fur, in vegetation or under rocks. Only domesticated (European) rabbits (brought here by the Dutch settlers) dig extensive burrows and warrens.

Rabbits and hares are coprophagous, meaning that they eat their poo. The thought may leave a bad taste in your mouth, but the method in this madness is that it allows for double digestion. Rabbits and

215

hares are mainly nocturnal, and feed on grass, leaves, roots and stems. This produces dark, soft faecal pellets that are eaten directly from the anus while the animal is at rest during the day. These pellets are then redigested so as to extract maximum nutrient value from the food. At night, they excrete hard, dry, light-coloured pellets.

Rodents and rabbits or hares?

Rabbits and hares were once classified as rodents, but that's changed. Today they are classified as lagomorphs (from the Greek *lagos*, meaning 'hare', and *morphe*, meaning 'form').

Lagomorphs have two pairs of incisors on the upper jaw (one behind the other), whereas rodents have only one pair. The incisors of lagomorphs and rodents never stop growing. They constantly have to gnaw on fibrous materials to keep the length of their incisors in check.

Furthermore, lagomorphs are strictly herbivorous, whereas rodents are omnivores.

A baboon spider and a tarantula?

None. 'Tarantula' is simply a name associated with large, hairy and usually ground-dwelling spiders. These spiders are called tarantulas in America (and also in East Africa). But in South Africa we call them baboon spiders, for some unfathomable reason. Using the term 'baboon' for anything other than a baboon is generally frowned upon, but I'm told that the reason for calling these spiders this name stems from the similarity between the spider's legs and the fingers of a baboon. Maybe?

The name 'tarantula' was originally derived from Italy. It was originally given to the Southern European wolf spider, *Lycosa tarantula*, after the town Taranto in Italy.

But there's more to the name. Tarantism is a form of hysteria that was seen in Italy around 500 years ago. It was thought to have resulted from the bite of the tarantula. The only cure, it was surmised, was frenzied dancing by the victim, hence the lively tarantella folk dance that is practised in Italy to this day.

The largest tarantula is the Goliath birdeater (*Theraphosa blondi*), found in South America. Their leg span is approximately 30 cm. Unlike the name suggests, they seldom eat birds – they're able to eat most prey that is smaller than them, including birds on rare occasions.

A glow-worm and a firefly?

Firstly, they're neither worms nor flies. They're beetles from the family Lampyridae (from the Greek *lampein*, which means 'to shine').

The male beetles have wings, and so they can fly – hence fireflies. The females are wingless – hence glow-worms.

Their glow-in-the-dark light (called bioluminescence) is generated through the interaction of a number of substances, including water, oxygen, a luminous chemical called luciferin and an enzyme called luciferase (from the Latin *lucifer*, meaning light-bearing). They've cleverly devised a way of emitting light on the darkest night to find a mate. Even cleverer is that the 'heat of their passion' is diminished because bioluminescence generates marginal heat energy (unlike a light bulb that glows white hot).

The adults don't feed, so they live only for a few days, relying on the energy reserves in their bodies that were accumulated during the larval stage, which feeds mainly on snails.

I wish I was a glow-worm
A glow-worm's never glum
'Cause how can you be grumpy
When the sun shines out your bum?

Different kinds of animal 'on the hoof', such as antelope, deer, buck, gazelle and duiker?

- **Antelopes and deer:** They are both ungulates (even-toed) and ruminants (with a four-chambered stomach – they chew the cud). But antelopes belong to the family Bovidae, whereas deer belong to the family Cervidae. An apparent difference between the two lies in the headgear: horns versus antlers. Antelope have hollow, unbranched and permanent horns. Deer have antlers, which are branched, and are grown and shed every year.

   There are no native deer in South Africa, although we do have fallow deer, introduced about 150 years ago. Only one species of deer occurs naturally in Africa, namely the Barbary stag or Atlas deer (in Algeria, Morocco and Tunisia).

- **Buck:** In the rest of the world, 'buck' is the name generally given to a male deer, antelope, sheep, hare, rabbit or rat. In South Africa, though, the term 'buck' is used as a generalisation for any antelope species (think about people saying 'We saw many buck in the park' or 'Their car struck a buck on the road'). Also, some of our antelope have the term as part of their name, for example, springbuck, reedbuck and bushbuck.

- **Gazelle:** This term is used to describe smaller African antelope (but not as small as duiker). Usually, but not always, both male and female gazelles have horns. Gazelles are also known for stotting or pronking, in which they jump high into the air with stiff legs and all four hooves off the ground at the same time. That's why impalas, even though they are a species of smaller antelope, are not considered gazelles: the females don't have horns and they don't stot. Springbuck, in contrast, *are* showy gazelles.

- **Duiker:** This is the name given to a subfamily of the smallest African antelopes. There are 18 species in this subfamily and substantially more subspecies. *Duiker* means 'diver' in Dutch, presumably after the way these small antelope dive into cover when they're making a headlong escape. Three species of duiker occur in South Africa, namely the common (grey) duiker, the red forest duiker and the blue duiker.

Collective nouns for animals

I've often heard heated differences of opinion on game drives about the 'correct' collective noun attributable to a particular group of animals.

More often than not, collective nouns describe the character, behaviour or personality of a group of animals, or are descriptive of their shape or character.

The first list of collective names for animals appeared in the 15th century in a book about hunting, hawking and heraldry. Over the ages, this new vocabulary applicable to groupings of animals grew. Many of the descriptive terms have remained in use for centuries. And, as can be expected, over time, certain species have been given different or additional collective nouns – as a survey of the literature will show. So, which name is correct, and which is incorrect?

There's no such thing as 'the right' or 'the wrong' collective noun, Alan Levine told me when we discussed his book *Alan Levine's Serendipity of Collective Nouns*. Years of dedicated research culminated in this unique volume, which deservedly earns him the title of the king of collective nouns.

Although there may well be popular, accepted or ancient collective nouns for particular groups of animals, Levine says, 'You're at liberty to call a group of animals anything that takes your fancy. That's the fun of it! And, many collective nouns are even descriptive in the context of what the group of animals is doing at the time.'

Take giraffes, for example, and some of their descriptive collective nouns in context. We get:

- a *corps* of giraffe – a small group together
- a *herd* of giraffe – describing a group, meaning one kind remaining together
- a *lope* of giraffe – a group walking

- a *journey* of giraffe – a group walking
- a *stretch* of giraffe – a group eating
- a *tower* of giraffe – a group with heads above trees
- a *troop* of giraffe – a group moving or resting
- a *neck* of giraffe – giraffes fighting.

Something similar happens with a group of hippos:
- a *crash* – a group of hippos on land
- a *pack* – a group of hippos on land
- a *pod* – a small group of hippos in water
- a *raft* – a group of hippos in water
- a *herd* – describing a group, meaning one kind remaining together
- a *bloat* – fanciful
- a *huddle* – fanciful
- a *snort* – fanciful
- a *wallow* – fanciful.

The point is, there's no right or wrong. 'The English language is alive, dynamic and ever-changing. New words arise all the time,' says Levine. His advice? 'Have fun with collective nouns!'

I must say, this changed my thinking somewhat, since I have often wondered (in an effort to stop the bickering on game drives) if there were 'more correct' or 'most correct' collective nouns for the well-known South African animals.

I've compiled a list of collective nouns selected out of the plethora of terms that are, or can be, used for a particular bunch of animals. Most are mentioned in Levine's book and some may be new to you. This is simply my take on the collective nouns in use for some of the South African wildlife that we know. I have not 'invented' any in the list. Some names are obvious, some defy understanding, and many are simply charming.

Aardvark – an *armoury* of aardvark
Ants – an *army* or *colony* of ants

Baboons – a *troop, tribe, congress* or *flange* of baboons

Bats – a *belfry, colony* or *cloud* of bats

Buffaloes – a *herd, obstinacy* or *gang* of buffalo

Butterflies – a *kaleidoscope* or *flutter* of butterflies

Chameleons – a *camouflage* of chameleons

Cheetahs – a *coalition* of cheetah

Cobras – a *quiver* of cobras

Cockroaches – an *intrusion* of cockroaches

Cormorants – a *gulp* of cormorants

Cranes – a *sedge* of cranes

Crocodiles – a *congregation* of crocodiles, or a *bask* (on land) or a *float* (in water)

Crowned or blacksmith lapwings – a *deceit* of lapwings

Crows – a *murder* of crows

Dolphins – a *pod* or a *school* of dolphins

Doves – a *dole* or a *pitying* of doves

Ducks – a *flock* of ducks (in flight), a *badling* (on the ground), a *paddling* or a *raft* (on water)

Eagles – a *convocation* or an *aerie* of eagles

Elephants – a *parade, memory* or *herd* of elephants

Finches – a *charm* of finches

Flamingos – a *flamboyance* or a *stand* of flamingos

Frogs – a *knot* of frogs

Giraffes – a *tower* of giraffes (see more examples earlier)

Guinea fowls – a *confusion* or a *rasp* of guinea fowl

Hedgehogs – an *array* of hedgehogs

Herons – a *siege, sedge* or *hedge* of herons

Hippopotamuses – a *raft, pod* or *bloat* of hippos (see more examples earlier)

Honey badgers – a *cete* or *colony* of honey badgers

Hyenas – a *pack, clan* or *cackle* of hyenas

Impalas – a *leap* or *herd* of impalas

Jackals – a *skulk* of jackal

Jellyfish – a *smack* of jellyfish

Larks – an *exaltation* of larks

Leopards – a *leap*, *prowl* or *spot* of leopards
Leverets (baby hares) – a *kindle* of leverets
Lions – a *pride* or *assault* of lions
Lizards – a *lounge* of lizards
Mice – a *mischief* of mice
Mongooses – a *forage* or *business* of mongooses
Monkeys – a *shrewdness* of monkeys (I also came across a *cartload* of monkeys)
Mosquitoes – a *scourge* of mosquitoes
Owls – a *parliament*, *stare* or *wisdom* of owls
Parrots – a *pandemonium* of parrots
Porcupines – a *prickle* of porcupines
Ravens – an *unkindness* of ravens
Rhinos – a *crash* of rhinos
Scorpions – a *bed* or *nest* of scorpions
Seagulls – a *flotilla*, *screech* or *squabble* of seagulls
Sharks – a *shiver* of sharks
Snakes – a *slither* of snakes
Spiders – a *cluster* or *clutter* of spiders
Springbuck – a *leap* or *herd* of springbuck
Starfish – a *constellation* of starfish
Starlings – a *murmuration* of starlings
Storks – a *mustering* of storks
Swallows – a *flight* of swallows
Tortoises – a *creep* of tortoises
Tree squirrels – a *scurry* of tree squirrels
Turtles – a *turn* of turtles
Vultures – a *kettle* of vultures when circling, a *committee* when perched, a *wake* when feeding on a carcass
Warthogs – a *sounder* of warthogs
Wild dogs – a *pack* of wild dogs
Wildebeest – a *herd* or *implausibility* of wildebeest
Zebras – a *dazzle* or *zeal* of zebra

South Africa's protected areas

Contrary to belief, it's not only national parks that form the protected areas of South Africa. Apart from national parks and nature reserves, protected areas also include forest nature reserves, forest wilderness areas, mountain catchment areas and World Heritage Sites. South Africa has around 1 500 protected areas, the most of any country in sub-Saharan Africa.

There is over 11 million hectares (approximately 112 000 km²) of protected land in South Africa. To put this into perspective, the total land area is about the same size as Cuba, and bigger than countries such as Portugal or Denmark. And if all the protected land in South Africa were lumped together to form a province of its own, a Protected Land Province, it would be bigger than the North-West, KwaZulu-Natal, Mpumalanga or Gauteng.

This all sounds very impressive, you may think, but is it enough? The number of protected areas is not the same as the percentage of land area of a country that is under protection. As a percentage, it's certainly not in line with the extent to which other countries in the world are protecting their 'special' areas.

According to the World Database on Protected Areas, Seychelles is at the top of the list, protecting 61% of its land area. Zambia is eleventh on the list, with 41% of protected land area, Tanzania comes in eighteenth, with 38% protected, and Namibia is in nineteenth place, with 37% of land area protected. South Africa is 139th on the list, with only 8% of its land area protected.

Nevertheless, South Africa is revered worldwide for the magnificent wildlife and scenery in its spectacular parks and reserves. The purpose of national parks is to protect and conserve animals, plants and their habitats for the future, and to provide an opportunity for people to experience and enjoy the natural wonders of our planet. South Africa has 19 national parks as well as a number of provincial reserves and wilderness areas.

Here are a few lesser-known snippets about some of our parks and reserves, and an explanation of their names.

Addo Elephant National Park

Addo means 'poison ravine'. The name derives from the Khoisan, who probably named it after the poisonous euphorbia plants that grow there. The San used the sap of poisonous euphorbias to poison their arrows. Only steenbok and klipspringer are known to (be able to) eat euphorbias.

The Addo Elephant National Park was proclaimed in 1931 to protect the last 11 elephants that remained after the wildlife in the area had been decimated by hunters since the 1700s.

Addo is home to the Big Seven: elephant, lion, rhino, leopard, buffalo, southern right whales and the great white shark.

Agulhas National Park

Agulhas means 'needles' in Portuguese. About 500 years ago, Portuguese mariners called this place Cabo das Agulhas – Cape of Needles. They noticed that there was no magnetic deviation here; the compass needle (magnetic north) coincided with true north in this region.

It's also possible that the name 'Agulhas' may be derived from the deadly, needle-like rocks that thrust up from the seabed in this region, and which are responsible for the many shipwrecks that have occurred there over the years.

/Ai/Ais–Richtersveld Transfrontier Park

/Ai/Ais derives from the Nama word /Ae-/aes, meaning 'fire-fire'. It refers to the 'burning water' of the hot springs (with a temperature of around 60 °C). The Richtersveld part is named after the Reverend W Richter, a missionary in northern Namaqualand in the 1840s.

Augrabies Falls National Park

Augrabies means 'place of the great noise', a derivation from the

Khoisan word *aukoerebis*, after the thundering, 56-m high waterfall on the Orange River, the largest in South Africa.

Bontebok National Park

By the early 1800s, hunters had all but wiped out bontebok in the south-western Cape, their natural habitat; at one stage there were only 17 individuals left. Amazingly for those times, it was a handful of farmers who took action when they realised the demise of the species was imminent. The Van der Byl, Van Breda and Albertyn families set aside portions of their farmland as 'safe areas' to protect the bontebok. If it weren't for their foresight at the time, the bontebok might well be extinct today, like the quagga.

The first Bontebok National Park was proclaimed in 1931 on land near Bredasdorp. The park was later moved to Swellendam to better suit the habitat requirements of the bontebok.

The Bontebok National Park is the smallest of the South African national parks, but it has the highest density of rare and endangered fynbos and bird and animal life. At 28 km², it can comfortably support only around 200 bontebok. By the 1970s, the worldwide population of bontebok had grown to 800. Today it's estimated that the worldwide population of this species is around 3 000, all derived from the original population in the Bontebok National Park.

Camdeboo National Park

Camdeboo means 'green hollow' in Khoisan. The Camdeboo National Park showcases the unique beauty, landscapes and ecosystems of the ancient Great Karoo. The historic town of Graaff-Reinet is almost completely surrounded by the Camdeboo National Park. Graaff-Reinet is the fourth-oldest town in South Africa and has more national monuments than any other town in the country.

Golden Gate Highlands National Park

The name refers to the spectacular shades of golden sunlight reflected off ochre and orange-hued sandstone cliffs in the park, the Brandwag buttress rock in particular – the most notable feature in the park.

Hluhluwe–iMfolozi Park

Formerly known as the Hluhluwe–Umfolozi Game Reserve, it's the oldest proclaimed nature reserve in South Africa, established in 1895. *Hluhluwe* is the isiZulu word for the thorny rope climber, *Dalbergia armata*. *iMfolozi* means 'zig-zag' in isiZulu, probably in reference to the course of the Umfolozi River.

iSimangaliso Wetland Park

The word *iSimangaliso* means 'a miracle' or 'something wonderous' in isiZulu. Apparently, an emissary of Shaka reported back to his king that what he saw in this area was a miracle. Central to the park is Lake St Lucia, the name given to the Tugela River mouth by the Portuguese in the 1500s (St Lucia was the patron saint of the blind, around 700 years ago). In 1822, the British proclaimed the area a town.

Karoo National Park

The word 'Karoo' implies 'thirstland', derived from the Khoi word *!'Aukarob*, meaning 'hard or dry'. It's also been suggested that 'karoo' may have been derived from the Khoi word *garo*, meaning 'desert'.

Kgalagadi Transfrontier Park

Kgalagadi means 'a waterless place'. The word 'Kalahari' is derived from the Setswana word *kgala*, which means 'great thirst', since the vast red sands of the Kalahari don't have permanent surface water. Because the southern Kalahari receives proportionally more rain, this region is often referred to as the green Kalahari.

Kruger National Park

Originally proclaimed the Sabie Game Reserve in 1898, it was renamed the Kruger National Park in 1926 after South African president Paul Kruger. Covering almost 20 000 km², it is 360 km long and 90 km across at its widest point. It is one of the largest wildlife parks in Africa – approximately the same size as Israel.

Mapungubwe National Park

Mapungubwe means 'hill (or place) of jackals', derived from the Tshivenda word *phunghuwe* for jackal. About a thousand years ago, Mapungubwe was the centre of the largest kingdom on the subcontinent. It was perhaps southern Africa's first state. The sophisticated, class-based society traded ivory and gold with China, India and Egypt. Mapungubwe is considered a precursor to Great Zimbabwe.

Marakele National Park

Marakele comes from the Setswana word meaning 'place of sanctuary'.

Mokala National Park

Mokala derives from the Setswana name for the signature tree in this park, the camel thorn (*Vachellia erioloba*).

Table Mountain National Park

In 1488, Bartolomeu Dias was the first European to set eyes on what is now known as Table Mountain. About 10 years later, in 1497, Vasco da Gama gazed upon it. Six years later, in 1503, it was climbed by the Portuguese mariner, Admiral Antonio de Saldanha, who named it Taboa da caba, meaning 'Table of the Cape'.

Tankwa Karoo National Park

The park is named after the Tankwa River that runs through the park, one of the most arid parts of South Africa. The origins of the word are uncertain: nobody knows what 'tankwa' really means. Some say that the word means 'turbid waters'.

References

Mammals

Carnaby T. 2012. *Beat about the Bush: Mammals*. Johannesburg: Jacana.

Cheung H, Mazerolle L, Possingham HP, Biggs D. 2018. Medicinal use and legalized trade of rhinoceros horn from the perspective of traditional Chinese medicine practitioners in Hong Kong. *Tropical Conservation Science* 2018:11.

Cloete OB, Kok G. 1986. Aspects of the water economy of Steenbok (*Raphicerus campestris*) in the Namib Desert. *Modqua* 14(4): 375–387.

Cornel AJ, Lee Y, Almeida APG, *et al.* 2018. Mosquito community composition in South Africa and some neighboring countries. *Parasites & Vectors* 11:331.

De Jong YA, D'Huart J-P, Butynski TM. 2023. Biogeography and conservation of desert warthog *Phacochoerus aethiopicus* and common warthog *Phacochoerus africanus* (Artiodactyla: Suidae) in the Horn of Africa. Mammalia 87(1):1–19.

Emmet M, Pattrick S. 2012. *Game Ranger in your Backpack*. Pretoria: Briza.

Fitzpatrick CL, Altmann J, Alberts SC. 2015. Exaggerated sexual swellings and male mate choice in primates: Testing the reliable indicator hypothesis in the Amboseli baboons. *Animal Behaviour* 104:175–185.

Mills G, Hes L. 1997. *Complete Book of Southern African Mammals*. Cape Town: Struik.

Schmitt M, Stears K, Shrader A. 2016. Zebra reduce predation risk in mixed-species herds by eavesdropping on cues from giraffe. *Behavioral Ecology* 27(4):1073–1077.

Smithers R. 1983. *The Mammals of the Southern African Subregion*. Pretoria: University of Pretoria.

Turner JA, Vasicek CA, Somers MJ. 2015. Effects of a colour variant on hunting ability: The white lion in South Africa. *Open Science Repository Biology* Online:e45011830.

Wang S-Q, Ye J, Meng J, *et al.* 2022. Sexual selection promotes giraffoid head-neck evolution and ecological adaptation. *Science* 376(6597). https://doi.org/10.1126/science.abl8316.

Birds
Brown CJ, Plug I. 1990. Food choice and diet of the bearded vuture *Gypaetus barbatus* in southern Africa. *South African Journal of Zoology* 25(3):169–177.

Ryan P. 2013. Underwater heron: African darter. *African Birdlife* Jul/Aug 2013:55–60.

Sinclair I, Hockey P, Tarboton W, Ryan P. 2011. *Sasol Birds of Southern Africa*. Cape Town: Struik Nature.

Weihs D, Katzir G. 1994. Bill sweeping in the spoonbill, *Platalea leucorodia*: Evidence for a hydrodynamic function. *Animal Behaviour* 47(3):649–654.

Reptiles and amphibians
Branch B. 1998. *Field Guide to the Snakes and Other Reptiles of Southern Africa*. Cape Town: Struik.

Christensen CB, Christensen-Dalsgaard J, Brand C, Madsen PT. 2012. Hearing with an atympanic ear: Good vibration and poor sound-pressure detection in the royal python, *Python regius. Journal of Experimental Biology* 215 (Pt 2):331–342.

Henderson DM. 2003. Effects of stomach stones on the buoyancy and equilibrium of a floating crocodilian: A computational analysis. *Canadian Journal of Zoology* 81(8):1346–1357.

Herbert SS, Hayes WK. 2009. Denim clothing reduces venom expenditure by rattlesnakes striking defensively at model human limbs. *Annals of Emergency Medicine* 54(6):830–836.

Marais J. 2022. *A Complete Guide to the Snakes of Southern Africa*. Cape Town: Struik Nature.

Miller AK, Maritz B, McKay S, Glaudas X, Alexander GJ. 2015. An ambusher's arsenal: Chemical crypsis in the puff adder (*Bitis arietans*). Proceedings of the Royal Society B 282:20152182.

Pietersen D, Jansen R, Swart J, Kotze A. 2016. *A conservation assessment of Smutsia temminckii*. In: Child MF, Roxburgh L, Do Linh San E, Raimondo D, Davies-Mostert HT, eds. *The Red List of Mammals of South Africa, Swaziland and Lesotho*. Pretoria: South African National Biodiversity Institute.

Westhoff G, Boetig M, Bleckmann H, Young BA. 2010. Target tracking during venom 'spitting' by cobras. *Journal of Experimental Biology* 213(11):1797–1802.

Arthropods

Evans MEG. 1972. The jump of the click beetle (Coleoptera, Elateridae) – a preliminary study. *Journal of Zoology* 167(3):319–336.

Holm E. 2008. *Insectlopedia of Southern Africa*. Pretoria: LAPA.

Holm E, Dippenaar-Schoeman A. 2010. *Goggo Guide: The arthropods of Southern Africa*. Pretoria: LAPA.

Picker M, Griffiths C, Weaving A. 2004. *Field Guide to the Insects of South Africa*. Cape Town: Struik.

Plants

Dyer C. 2014. New names for the African *Acacia* species in *Vachellia* and *Senegalia*. *Southern Forests* 76(4):iii.

Nsuala B, Enslin G, Viljoen A. 2015. "Wild cannabis": A review of the traditional use and phytochemistry of *Leonotis leonurus*. *Journal of Ethnopharmacology* 174:520–539.

Schmidt E, Lotter M, McCleland W. 2002. *Trees and Shrubs of Mpumalanga and Kruger National Park*. Johannesburg: Jacana.

South African National Biodiversity Institute. PlantZAfrica. http://pza.sanbi.org.

Van Wyk B, Van Wyk P. 1997. *Field Guide to Trees of Southern Africa*. Cape Town: Struik.

General

Levine A. 2007. *Alan Levine's Serendipity of Collective Nouns: Creatures Big & Small*. Penryn Press.

Linnean Society. Who was Linnaeus? https://www.linnean.org/learning/who-was-linnaeus.

South African National Parks. SANParks. https://www.sanparks.org.

Watt R. 1999. *VeldFocus: Ten Years of Nature's Wonders*. Centurion: Rapid Commercial Print.

Acknowledgements

I am deeply indebted to the following people, without whom this book would not have seen the light of day:

Annie Olivier, publishing director of Jonathan Ball Publishers, for giving me the opportunity to write this book, for instilling the confidence in me to do so and for her encouragement whenever I needed it.

Linda Pretorius, science writer and editor, whose 'pedantometer' permanently red-lined to keep me firmly on the scientific straight and narrow, her remarkable insight and interpretation helping to replot routes when the manuscript strayed off course. Your piece on biological classification is integral to this book. Thank you again, Linda.

Nicole Duncan, editor at Jonathan Ball Publishers, for her calm demeanour, endless patience and welcome reassurance when the chips were down.

Johan Marais, South Africa's herpetologist extraordinaire and a long-time friend, for planting the seed – 'It's time you expressed yourself in a book,' he said – and making it happen by introducing me to Annie Olivier. Thank you too, Johan, for your guidance and generous support with images and specialised insight into the content.

My sincerest thanks also to Ashley Kemp, Bernard Wooding, Prof. Claire Spottiswoode, Lindsey Kernodle, Vincent Cornelissen and Dr Yvonne de Jong for the images you have provided so generously.

And to Benn and Ladoo, Clay, Keegs and Paulie for your belief and encouragement. And thank you for listening so patiently when I say too much . . .

Image acknowledgements

P6   *Female baboon in estrus*: D. Gordon E. Robertson

P12   *The Big Five*: Elephant: Ikiwaner; lion: Yathin S Krishnappa; buffalo: Gouldingken; rhino: Richard Ruggiero; leopard: Steve Jurvetson/ Creative Commons Attribution

P13   *The Small Five*: Elephant shrew: Chris and Mathilde Stuart; red-billed buffalo weaver: Greg Tee; rhino beetle: Bernard Dupont; antlion: Yakovlev Alexey; leopard tortoise: Bernard Dupont

P20   *Elephant foreheads comparison*: Quinton Coetzee

P27   *Large spotted genet*: Bernard Dupont *African civet*: I've Got It On Film!

P44   *Carnivore family tree*: Quinton Coetzee

P45   *Aardwolf*: Dominik Käuferle *Striped hyena*: Rushikesh Deshmukh DOP

P56   *Shrew caravan*: Photaro

P60   *Rau quaggas*: The Quagga Project

P71   *Desert warthog*: Thomas M. Butynski & Yvonne A. de Jong

P85   *Whiffling goose*: Vincent Cornelissen Photography

P98   *Flamingo's centre of gravity*: Quinton Coetzee

P99   *Green-backed heron*: GerifalteDelSabana

P103   *Honeyguide hatchling's lethal bill-hooks*: Clair Spottiswoode

P112   *African spoonbill*: Bernard Dupont

P113   *Spur-winged goose*: Luis Agassiz Fuertes

P124   *Chameleon catching prey*: Ashley Kemp

P126   *Chameleon's tongue components*: Quinton Coetzee

P127   *Chameleon eyes*: Johan Marais

P136   *Boomslang*: Johan Marais *Black mamba*: Johan Marais

P139   *Snouted cobra*: Johan Marais

P140   *How snakes swallow large prey*: Lindsey Kernodle Artwork

P142   *Common egg eater eating a bird egg*: Johan Marais *Common egg eater regurgitating an egg shell*: Johan Marais

P143   *Common egg eater and common night adder*: Johan Marais *Sundevall's shovel-snout*: Johan Marais

P146   *Rinkhals feigning death*: Johan Marais

P148   *Mozambique spitting cobra*: Johan Marais

P149   *Puff adder*: Johan Marais

P150   *Bibron's stiletto snake*: Johan Marais

P153   *Boomslang showing the position of the back fangs*: Johan Marais

P154   *Cape cobra*: Johan Marais

P155   *Tutankhamun's mask*: Mark Fischer

P156   *Venom direction of a non-spitter and a spitter*: Quinton Coetzee

P175   *Antlion larva*: Bogomaz Mykhailo *Antlion pit traps*: Cyron Ray Macey

P183   *Death's-head hawkmoth*: Gail Hampshire *Death's-head hawkmoth caterpillar*: Erik Streb

P185   *Earwig*: Rainer Altenkamp

P189   *Mopane worms*: SAplants

P190   *Mopane emperor moth*: Bernard Dupont

P 194   *Scorpion under UV light*: Polina Razumova

P196   *Black button spider*: Johan Marais

P197   *Brown button spider*: Johan Marais *Violin spider*: Johan Marais

P198   *Sac spider*: Ashley Kemp *Baboon spider*: Ashley Kemp

P199   *Jumping spider*: Ashley Kemp

P200   *Daddy long-legs spider*: Ashley Kemp

P205   *Sagole Baobab*: Scott Davies

P206   *Cork bush*: SAplants

P210   *Giant stapelia flower*: Canglesea

P212   *Wild dagga*: Harvey Barrison

About the author

QUINTON COETZEE is a naturalist, an international speaker, an entrepreneur and an adventurer with a deep passion for wild creatures and wild places.

He is considered one of Southern Africa's leading bushcraft and survival specialists. Quinton is also well known as a presenter for popular television wildlife programmes such as *Aardwolf* and *50/50 Veldfocus*.

Quinton has a BSc degree from Rhodes University and is a former director at the Johannesburg Zoo.

He is also a classical pianist and lives in White River.